JESUS,
TAKE THE
DRIVER'S
SEAT

AMBA ONOCHIE

Jesus, Take the Driver's Seat

Trilogy Christian Publishers
A Wholly Owned Subsidary of Trinity Broadcasting Network
2442 Michelle Drive
Tustin, CA 92780

For information, address Trilogy Christian Publishing

Rights Department, 2442 Michelle Drive, Tustin, CA 92780.

Trilogy Christian Publishing/ TBN and colophon are trademarks of Trinity Broadcasting Network.

For information about special discounts for bulk purchases, please contact Trilogy Christian Publishing.

10 9 8 7 6 5 4 3 2 1

Library of Congress Cataloging-in-Publication Data is available.

ISBN 979-8-89041-987-3

ISBN 979-8-89041-988-0 (ebook)

INTRODUCTION

Amba Ministries is focused on general intercessory breakthrough prayers, healing, counseling, deliverance, and mentoring under the guidance of the Holy Spirit. I received some training in Canada, where I served the Lord in different intercessory prayer groups, women's prayer ministry, as well as the healing and deliverance ministry at Calvary Worship Center in Surrey, BC.

The Lord encouraged me to return to school so that I might teach more effectively, so I enrolled at Liberty University Seminary and obtained a Master of Arts in Theological Studies by the grace of God in December of 2022.

I had a spiritual encounter with the Lord in 2006 at a Catholic Charismatic prayer meeting in

San Diego, California, where I lived for nearly ten years with my family. The Lord waited for the right moment to deliver and cleanse me, bringing me out of deep darkness into His marvelous Light before He could use me as His servant. The Lord said, "You are now a chicken without feathers, flesh, nor skin—just bony, for the Lord." Deep cleaning.

I thought it was all over, but no, I am currently going through a fiery furnace situation. I said, "How can I survive this painful fire?" Just when I thought it was over, I was put back into the fire. Later, the Lord showed me a beautiful fresh cleaned out baby that came out from the fire—will that be me?

Amba, a broken woman, who was physically and verbally abused, received my transformation and deliverance at God's time, for His Glory.

The Lord, in His great mercy and grace, taught, guided, instructed, and mentored me, and the Lord has continued to this day. The Lord also taught me how to use His Word to pray for myself, and especially for others (a gift from the Lord).

As a servant of God, I am very committed and

believe that God's Word is the ultimate wisdom and should always be proclaimed during prayers. The Lord said, "Use My Word to get more or all of My attention." What a manner of LOVE! Praise the Lord!

The Lord also gave me the opportunity to travel widely to places such as: Port Hardy in Canada, Qoas and Sao Paulo in Brazil, Bangalore in India, and Nigeria, proclaiming the good news and the love of Jesus Christ. In these areas, I visited several poor villages and preached the Gospel and helped to baptize a lot of individuals. Many received healing and deliverance in these countries and received Jesus as their Lord and Savior.

Acts 1:8 declares, "But you will receive power when the Holy Spirit comes upon you; and you shall be witnesses to Me in Jerusalem, and in all Judea and Samaria, and to the end of the earth."

I also visited orphanages in Bangalore, India, and a home for the widows where I had the opportunity to donate some food such as rice, schoolbooks, bags, clothing, spices, and money; to God be the Glory, many of these individuals accepted Christ and thus have been set free. All glory to God.

The Lord also blessed me with the opportunity in these countries through His teachings in the Scriptures to encourage individuals who have been hurt to forgive. I used my own path and experiences as a testimony, along with God's Word as an example, because unforgiveness causes barriers to progress and gives spirits of infirmities dominion over one's life. In one of my meetings in Bangalore, the Holy Spirit gave me the following to proclaim: "I am one crying in the wilderness for forgiveness." How sad. Although it is not easy to forgive, it takes patience and prayer, along with wisdom, but the Lord is always there to help us.

CHAPTER 2

A NOTE FROM
MY MENTOR

I am Pastor Rosemond Owusu, and I Pastor a church alongside my husband, who is the Senior Pastor. I have known Amba since 2015, when she first joined the Church after she moved from the United States to Surrey British Columbia, Canada.

Shortly after joining the Church, Amba expressed interest in the Women's Ministry in the Church, of which I am the leader.

She was committed to the Ministry and was serving in the area of prayer.

My Husband and I stepped up to mentor her with the guidance of the Holy Spirit. Amba had a desire to seek God and know Him more. Months after, she had an encounter with the Lord Jesus Christ that transformed her life and character drastically. During this encounter, she also received from the Lord a gift of healing whereby she would pray for the sick and they would be healed in Jesus' name.

This Ministry of Healing took Amba to a Church in the Vancouver area under the guidance of Pastor Sandeep Alex, teaching women in the area of prayer. Her ministry also took her to India many times under the guidance of Pastor Matthew P. where she ministers to the body of Christ in several villages.

Another thing that came out of her, after her encounter with the Lord Jesus, was a heart of love and compassion for the needy. For example, at Amba's request, I drafted a letter to the managers of some grocery stores around Surrey and Delta, British Columbia, Canada. The stores included No-frills and Canadian Superstores, and she solicited these stores for donations; these donations were given to the poor and needy at the Church.

Matthew 25:35 declares, "For I was hungry, and you gave me food, I was thirsty, and you gave Me drink, I was a stranger, and you took Me in."

Gods Richest Blessing

Sincerely Yours

Pastor Rosemond Owusu

Director Of Women's Ministry.

CHAPTER 3:

MY LIFE, ABUSE, CONTROL, SIN, AND DISOBEDIENCE

I was about eighteen years of age when I got married to the first man who approached me for marriage, still in college; my mother said I should not get married too soon, but I ignored my mother's advice because he was very handsome and wealthy. My troubles/abuse began right after my marriage; there was much controlling, verbal abuse, and physical abuse. I was whipped with a belt, given scares on my shoulder and back, and kicked on my stomach; a bottle of alcohol was emptied on my head. I was kicked on my forehead, which resulted in much bleeding, because I visited a friend of mine next door. I still have the scar on my forehead, a blind right eye, which needed surgery because of the injury on my forehead, an aching ear, and loose teeth that needed dental implants, but after a few years, I managed to escape my abuser.

SURGERIES:

While living in Schaumburg, Illinois, I had tooth and gum issues because of the physical abuse. According to my dentist, I needed surgery because of my loose teeth and gum issues, and he suggested implants, which I did, but right after the implants, I moved to Surrey, British Columbia, where I lived for about four years before moving to Austin, Texas.

It was time to exchange my driver's license from a British Columbia to a Texas state license, but while reading the text or numbers at the DMV, I could not see clearly. It was extremely difficult to see any letter with my right eye. It was totally blind. The lady at the driver's license office insisted I must visit the ophthalmologist; well, I did, and surgery was suggested.

I prayed and wept while asking Jesus to heal me, but there was no response. I said, "Lord, You healed the sick through me, Your servant, You also healed all kinds of pain—the lame walked, blind eyes and deaf ears were also restored, so why will You not heal me?"

I prayed and knocked on heaven's door, but I was not healed by the Lord, so on the day of my surgery, I mentioned to the surgeon that my heart desire was for Jesus to heal me, but the surgeon said, "He has," because the Lord sent me to him. He is a Christian, and my surgery went well because I had no complications. God is good.

CHAPTER 4:

CONTROL

After my studies at a teacher's college, my first daughter was born, but the abuse got even worse. I was not allowed to have friends nor visit family members, and twice he drove out two of my friends who paid me a visit and sternly warned them never to return. Although I did not have any relationship with Jesus and was not prayerful, in my dreams I saw two persons or spirits who talked to one another; the one who wore white clothing yelled at the one who wore black clothing saying, "Leave her alone." I did not know what it meant at that time, but now I have come to realize it was Jesus yelling at the Devil to leave me alone. I have come to accept that all our troubles in this wicked evil wilderness we call home are caused by Satan and his agents.

Even when I was not saved, Jesus loved me.

He loved me when I was unlovable.

Jesus loved me while I was in Satan's territory, covered with his blanket of lies, deceit, blinded and muted, with no strength of mind and no will power.

Jesus loved me while I dwelt in Egypt with many enemies.

Jesus loved me even the years I roamed around the wilderness.

Jesus loved me when I did not truly know who He was, and Jesus loved me when I did not attend Church nor prayed.

CHAPTER 5:

GOD IS LOVE, SCRIPTURES

God loves all mankind regardless of our sins, for Scripture tells us, "Even when we were dead in trespasses, He made us alive together with Christ" (Ephesians 2:5).

John 3:16 tells us, "For God so loved the world that He gave His only begotten Son, that whoever believes in Him should not perish but have everlasting life." For "God is love" (1 John 3:8, NIV); "He loved us and sent His Son to be the propitiation for our sins" (1 John 3:10, NKJV); and "[n]ow in Christ Jesus we who once were far off have been brought near by the blood of Christ" (Ephesians 2:13, NKJV). "We are a chosen generation, a royal priesthood, a holy nation, His own special people, that you may proclaim the praises of Him who called you out of darkness into His marvelous light, who once were not a people but are now the people of God, who had not obtained mercy but now have obtained mercy" (1 Peter 2:9-10, NKJV). "For you were like sheep going astray but have now returned to the Shepherd and Overseer of your souls" (1 Peter 2:25, NKJV).

Please note: Jesus told me, "We are no longer in Satan's territory, we belong to Him because He has bought us back with His shed blood on the Cross." He paid a very "high prize." (1 Corinthians 6:20; 1 Corinthians 7:23). So, we are now His responsibility, His prized possession.

Thank you, Jesus, that we are sanctified, justified, redeemed, washed with the blood, and our sins are continually forgiven (1 Corinthians 6:11; Ephesians 1:8; 1 Corinthians 6:20).

Jesus said, "Amba, I brought you out from the darkness into My marvelous Light." He opened my eyes to see and know the truth, which had been hidden from me for decades, and unmuted me. What a manner of love, love that is so intense.

LOVE:

GOD INCARNATE, HE PUT ON FLESH, A HEART PROBLEM:

The crowds asked, "Who is this man? Who are You Jesus?"

He is the incarnate Son of the Most High God, the Almighty God, God the Son.

He is the Greatest King, the Greatest Lover, and the Lover of our souls who is still seeking His bride in villages, towns, and cities. Jesus came to seek our hearts and to win many lovers. He is searching for brides and making families, and Jesus came to reveal the Father to us. He is also seeking to have a close relationship with mankind, His children, His bride. If Jesus wakes you up at 3:30 am, will you be able to get up and spend time with Him? What a Lover, OH Sweet Precious Jesus!

God was made manifest because of the sins of the world, a heart problem.

He put on flesh and died on the cross to quench the Father's wrath on mankind, to satisfy God's wrath towards us because of His love that is so intense. For example, in the Old Testament, when the Israelites sinned against God, they were slain, but in the New Testament, when mankind sins and repents from their sins and asks for forgiveness, all is forgiven because of Jesus. The Father's love.

According to one of my Professors at the Seminary (Liberty University), "We are not in the Garden of Eden, because living in the garden did not produce godliness, so something changed, under Noah, the Ark and the flooding of the earth did not do it, something changed, we might go back to the Tower of Babel, also under Abraham, something changed" (Christopher Moody).

All the signs and wonders God performed in the land of Egypt did not do it for mankind. For example, frogs, lies, and flies abounded in their land, locust ate up their vegetations, River Nile was turned to blood and all the fish destroyed; they were inflicted with boils, God gave them hail for rain, and Egypt's first born was destroyed (Exodus Chapters 7,8,9,10 &11, NKJV); but all these did not do it for mankind. Parting the Red Sea and circling around the wilderness for forty years did not do it (Exodus chapter 14); "fiery serpents in the wilderness" (Numbers 21:4-9, NKJV) did not do it either.

The book of Exodus tells us in chapter 13 verse 21, "God lead the way at night by fire, and cloud by day," but the people were stiff necked—it did not work for them.

"God rained manna from heaven for 40 years" (Exodus Chapter 16); "He gave them water to drink from the Rock" (Exodus 17); "He opened the rock, and water gushed out; It ran in the dry places like a river" (Psalm 105:41, NKJV).

"God even opened the ground to swallow Korah, Dathan, Abiram, and their families" (Numbers 16:13). "Miriam was afflicted with leprosy" (Numbers 12:8). And stopping the flow of River Jordan (Joshua 3:13) also did not do it for mankind.

The walls of Jericho crashed in the presence of mankind (Joshua 5:13-6:27, NIV), and God fought Israel's battles, but they were still stiff necked. God had to take on flesh, because it is a heart problem; the root of every matter is a heart problem.

CHAPTER 6 :

EVERLASTING LOVE

God wants us to extend that love towards one another because love is of God. It is Kingdom policy, for Scripture says, "But above all these things put on love, which is the bond of perfection" (Colossians 3:14, NKJV). It is well pleasing to the Father.

"Love suffers long and is kind; love does not envy; love does not parade itself, is not puffed up; does not behave rudely, does not seek its own, is not provoked, thinks no evil; does not rejoice in iniquity, but rejoices in the truth; bears all things, believes all things, hopes all things, endures all things. Love never fails" (1 Corinthians 13:4-8, NKJV).

Do we truly have this kind of love towards each other? This kind of love that does not come with jealousy, gossiping, or anger?

This kind of love that comes from the heart

and is true? Real? Washing each other's feet with compassion? The kind that provides for the needy? Cares for one another in sickness and in health. It is written, "Abide faith, hope, love, these three; but the greatest of these is love" (1 Corinthians 13:13, NKJV).

Jesus has commanded mankind to love one another because love never fails.

> Where there is love, peace reigns.
> Where there is love, joy reigns.
> Where there is love,
> there is always laughter and gladness.
> Where there is love,
> there is no hatred, only peace.

For it is written, "You shall love your neighbor as yourself, love does no harm to a neighbor; therefore, love is the fulfillment of the law" (Romans 13:9-10, NKJV).

For Moses came with the law, but Jesus came with love. It is written, "Let no one seek his own, but each one the other's well-being" (1 Corinthians 10:24, NKJV); "Let each of you look out not only for his own interests, but also for the interests of others" (Philippians 2:4, NKJV); and, "Bear one another's burdens, and so fulfill the law of Christ" (Galatians 6:2, NKJV). This is true love. For example, 1 Corinthians 13 talks about love as a way of life, the way mankind must live, focusing on others as we are commanded. Love is one's way of life, imitating Christ.

Scripture tells us, "If I give all I possess to the poor and give over my body to hardship that I may boast, but do not have love, I gain nothing. Love is patient, love is kind. It does not envy, it does not boast, it is not proud. It does not dishonor others, it is not self-seeking, it is not easily angered, it keeps no record of wrongs. Love does not delight in evil but rejoices with the truth. It always protects, always trusts, always hopes, always perseveres. Love never fails. But where there are prophecies, they will cease; where there are tongues, they will be stilled; where there is knowledge, it will pass away" (1 Corinthians 13:3-8, NIV).

As Christians or mankind, do we only love the individuals that look like us? The ones that talk like us? The ones that wear their hair like us? The ones that have the color of our skin? No, Jesus commanded us to love one another, to imitate Him, He who laid down His life for mankind for the sake of love, for God is love, and He is the greatest Lover, Who will wake one up at about 3:30am to spend time with Him.

He once asked me in His sweet voice, "Are you still sleeping?" What a manner of love.

Christians who love the Lord must keep His commandment to love and do good by caring for others. Love is also the foundation for us in the Christian life. Churches must preach love more because 1 John 4:8 tells us that "God is love." Love is what the Lord has done for mankind, exemplified in His beautiful creation, the gravity around the planet earth, the sun and planet earth He has stationed at the right position. Miracles are also God's sign of love for mankind. His healings, deliverances, the air we breathe, the water we drink and bathe in, the Light of the world, and much more.

We must show our love by the actions we take. Jesus stated that we must love the Lord our God and our neighbors as ourselves (Matthew 22:39, NKJV).

LOVE IS THE ANSWER:

Moses came with the Law,
but Jesus came with Love.

The Law is the beginning and end of the Old Testament, but Love is the beginning and end of the New Testament.

Love is the solution.

Love is the answer.

The truth is Love,

True, tender Love, which is the end of the Law.

Love with a heart of compassion and not hate.

Amen.

CHAPTER 7:

HUMILITY

Jesus came with total humility: "He was born in a room for animals, laid on a bed for animals, and wrapped with clothing for animals" (Luke 2:7). My former professor Christopher Moody affirmed, "Jesus removed His royal robes, royal crown, royal rings, and sandals" and stepped down into this wicked evil wilderness we call home for the "sake of love" (John 3:16) and our eternal life. He came to seek His bride: you and me.

Jesus walked through villages, towns, and cities, looking for His bride. He is still patiently searching for His bride. Jesus' hands are stretched out towards you and me. Please accept Jesus as your Bridegroom, our first True Love, our only True Love, Sweet Precious Jesus, for no one can love us the way Jesus does. Scripture tells us,

"Abraham rejoiced to see His day" (John 8:56–58, NKJV). Jesus said, before Abraham, I AM. Moses also asked God in the burning bush, if the people question who sent him, what shall he say? God answered to tell His people, "I AM WHO I AM...I AM has sent me to you" (Exodus 3:14, NIV).

Again, Jesus asked the people in the garden when He was about to be arrested, "Whom do you seek?" They said, "Jesus," and Jesus said, "I AM" (John 18:4–5, ESV). What does this mean? We now know who descended into this wicked wilderness we call home to die for our sins. What a manner of love. The One who was born by a virgin as planned by the Lord came with total humility.

God Himself died on the cross for our sins.
God Himself shed His blood for our sins.
God Himself allowed His body to be bruised from head to toe.
God allowed Himself to be naked.
God allowed Himself to suffer hunger and thirst.
God allowed Himself to be nailed on the cross.
His love is so intense.

JESUS, TAKE THE DRIVER'S SEAT

Thank You so much, Sweet Precious Jesus, for buying us back from Satan's territory at a "High Price" (1 Corinthians 6:20; 1 Corinthians 7:23). We are Yours Jesus.

CHAPTER 8:

THE HEART
OF STONE

Please give God a chance to sprinkle clean water on you; allow Him to remove the heart of stone from your flesh and give you a heart of flesh, to give you a clean heart, and put His Spirit within you, for it is a heart problem. Scripture tells us, "I will sprinkle clean water on you, and you shall be clean; I will cleanse you from all your filthiness and from all your idols. I will give you a new heart and put a new spirit within you; I will take the heart of stone out of your flesh and give you a heart of flesh. I will put My Spirit within you and cause you to walk in My statutes, and you will keep My judgments and do them" (Ezekiel 36:25-27, NKJV).

- What have you been able to let go of regarding your character?

- Have you been able to let go of pride?
- Have you been able to let go of verbal abuse? Physical abuse?
- Lies? Condescending ways? Gossip? Anger?
- Question: What have you been able to let go of?
- Are you able to forgive? Forgiveness is for you, and not for them, so please let go.

Lord, "What is mankind that You are mindful of them, human beings that You care for them?" (Psalm 8:4, NIV). "Lord, what are human beings that you care for them, mere mortals that you think of them?" (Psalm 144:3, NIV). "What is mankind that you make so much of them, that you give them so much attention, (Job 7:17, NIV). "What is mankind that you are mindful of them, a son of man that You care for him? You made them a little lower than the angels; You crowned them with glory and honor and put everything under their feet" (Hebrews 2:6-8, NIV).

GOD RAISES THE LOWLY, THE DOWNCAST, AND THE POOR:

Whatever you are going through in life is not permanent, so please "cling on to the Lord"

(Jeremiah 13:11) for He is our Helper. Do not give up, for your prayers will surely be answered. Jesus never turns a blind eye on the needy, so please surrender all to Him and wait patiently, for "His burden is light" (Matthew 11:30, NIV). I surrendered my heart to the Lord.

Jesus will send someone to help you because He is a good Father; Psalm 72:12 says, "For He will deliver the needy when he cries, the poor also, and him who has no helper" (NKJV). For "He raises the poor out of the dust, and lifts the needy out of the ash heap, that He may seat him with princes, with princes of His people" (Psalm 113:7–8, NKJV). Again, the Scripture says, Jesus "Raises the poor from the dust, and lifts the beggar from the ash heap, to set him among princes and make them inherit the throne of glory" (1Samuel 2:8, NKJV).

TESTIMONY:

During a regular Friday night prayer at Calvary Worship Center in Surrey, Canada, the Lord asked a sister to tell me, "He will lift you up because you have suffered so much in your life. You have been trampled upon, mocked, looked down on, and abused," and from that time onwards, He did as promise, step by step and slowly, for the things of the Kingdom are slow, the things of God are slow. I do remember my very first mission trip to Bangalore, India, as an evangelist; the Lord took over the messages. He downloaded them to me. He also took over the preaching, the many healings, and the deliverances He also took over. At each mission trip to Bangalore, many were healed and the lame walked; all kinds of pain were also healed.

HE IS AN EXCELLENT FATHER:

Do not be discouraged. Please pray and seek Him diligently, for our Father loves the poor and looks out for them. He will surely send someone to help you, for He is a Loving Father. Please do not look at what you are going through but look out for others, and God will come through for you. A few years ago, while living in British Columbia, Canada, the Lord asked me to visit managers of some grocery stores for donations. So, gift vouchers were given to me every three months, which was given to the poor in the

Church, and that is who God is: a very loving Father who will never forget the needy.

We serve a God who genuinely cares for the poor and the needy—so full of love. Please put your hope and trust in Him, for He is our Door of Hope, the Faithful One who never fails. He carried the cross for love's sake; why would He not listen and answer your prayers?

TESTIMONY:

The Lord said that He raised me from the sheepfold to become His servant and that I have received the covenant of David. He also brought me out from the darkness into His marvelous light. He lifted me from the floor because I have been trampled upon right from when I was eighteen years old, downcast (heartbroken, crushed, grief-stricken, depressed) physically, and verbally abused, mocked, given a blind right eye, broken forehead, many stripes on my body, and four loose teeth. I have also gone through hunger and thirst.

So, my brothers and sisters in Christ Jesus, what are you going through? What have you gone through?

God said, "Amba come, I will lift you up
because you have suffered so much."

My life is a wonderful example of what the Lord is capable of doing when one surrenders to Him, for I am just like Moses, a stammerer, one who is poor in speech, and a sinner. But the Lord decided to do something powerful with my life for His glory. This is the grace of God, the love of God, and the Kingdom of God.

Apostle James tells us, "Listen, my beloved brethren: Has God not chosen the poor of this world to be rich in faith and heirs of the kingdom which He promised to those who love Him?" (James 2:5, NKJV). Do you genuinely love the Lord? "For you see your calling, brethren, that not many wise according to the flesh, not many mighty, not many noble, are called. But God has chosen the foolish things of the world to put to shame the wise, and God has chosen the weak things of the world to put to shame the things which are mighty" (1 Corinthians 1:26-27, NKJV).

CHAPTER 9:

MY ESCAPE

I managed to escape my abuser and traveled out of the country to another country, but after a few years, I met another abuser and continued living in Egypt. The abuse and wilderness years continued shortly after we got married, and I was covered with Satan's blanket of lies, blindness, muteness, deceit, and much more.

SATAN'S WICKEDNESS:

I did not know the Devil could mute and blind one so badly. One can continue living with an abuser and stay abused and hurt, but the Lord set me free. So, after three little children, we moved from nation to nation, city to city due to my husband's job as a software engineer, and in each city or nation, furniture was left behind due to the cost of shipping, which is the Devil's way of stealing one's finances. I circled around the wilderness for forty years, lived with demons that tormented me and witches with big bags that stole my finances, peace, and joy. I had sleepless nights for about four years, and during that period, a relative of mine tried for several years to kill me but failed because of the grace of God upon my life. I found myself in a pit, like a water-well several times, but each time, strange people pulled me out. I once heard this relative's voice in my bedroom; not knowing how to pray, I did not pray much. My prayer was praise and worship, but God in His Mercy that is so rich came through for me. He did not allow this relative to kill me, and he died a few years ago.

HOW I MET THE LORD:

My husband is Catholic, and I occasionally attended Church with him. So, one fine day, he said we should attend a Charismatic healing service. It was during the service I met the Lord. A lady prayed and laid hands on me, which changed my life. I had such a hunger for the Lord that is unexplainable. I began to evangelize and continued to worship the Lord because praise and worship was my way of prayer.

GOD'S SCHOOL:

Shortly after I got saved, my family and I moved to British Columbia, where I joined a church that believed in intercessory prayers, so prayers were held daily at the church. Thank God for Calvary Worship Center Surrey, where I learned how to pray. After two years with the church, Jesus lifted me, trained me, guided, mentored, and allowed me to see and live with demons and witches.

God cannot give one a gift of healing and deliverance without an intense training, He will let you go through trials, be allowed to see the demons and witches; it is to strengthen you, to deliver you from fear of the demons, and to build a character in you. For example, a lady in one of the villages I visited during ministry in Bangalore, India, cried out—the spirit in her cried out, saying "Do not touch me, I have lived in her for several years." If God had not trained me, I would have left that meeting instantly due to fear, but because of my training, all fear was gone—from Amba, the one who was always afraid.

MINISTRY AND GIFTS:

The Lord told me that He waited for so many years to clean me before He could use me. He lifted a full-size chicken without feathers, skin, nor flesh, just bones. I am now that chicken without feathers, skin nor flesh, just bony for Jesus because I surrendered my heart to Him. I thought it was all over, but no, I am currently going through a fiery furnace situation. I said, "How can I survive this painful fire?" Just when I thought it was over, I was put back into the fire. Later, the Lord showed me a beautiful, fresh, cleaned-out baby that came out from the fire—will that be me?

God's desire is for us to be transformed to be Christ-like, because Christianity is change. I have traveled to Bangalore, India, about four times for ministry; to Qoas, Brazil, Port Hardy, which is the remote areas of Canada where some individuals still worship the sun and moon; also to Nigeria for women ministry. Many were healed of pain (shoulder, knee, and back pains), the lame walked, blind eyes were restored, and many were delivered from demons.

It was during a women's weekend retreat I noticed God had given me a gift of healing and deliverance. My hands were constantly hot, and my Pastor said I needed a mentor, and I was mentored by him.

GOD STARTED HIS HEALING WITH MY SON:

One of my sons returned from a basketball game with a dislocated knee; his coach made mention he might need surgery. Well, returning home from the retreat, I saw my son in so much pain, so laying hands on his knee, I commanded healing in the name of our Lord Jesus Christ, and he was instantly healed. Many also received healing in India, USA, Nigeria, and Canada. The Lord blessed or opened barren wombs, unsellable homes were sold, there were breakthrough prayers, and much more.

So many of us including myself try to hide who we are, our past mistakes, but God builds His Kingdom with the wounded and those who are broken. Yes, some pastors seek individuals who are eloquent in speech, but note that Apostle Paul was poor in speech, and he was teased by some, but he wrote most of the New Testament. Moses was poor in speech, but God sent him to lead the children of Israel out of Egypt. The Holy Spirit said in one of my meetings in India that I am Moses. Some individuals who are close to me abused me saying I am a stammerer, I am worthless and a fool, but God uses the unusable. My life is truly an example of what God can do when you surrender to Him.

Brothers and sisters, our suffering is not permanent because 1 Peter 5:10 tells us, "After we have suffered a while, God will perfect us, He will establish us, He will strengthen and settle us" (NKJV). He will do in accordance with His Word because He is a good Father.

The Lord said,

> "Amba, I am the God that settles.
> I am the God that establishes.
> I am the God that perfects,
> And the God that strengthens,"

but we must trust in Him.

He will also open the door of success, for He is

the Door and the only Way. Please put your hope in Him, delight in Him, fear Him, love Him, and have faith in Him, for He will surely come through.

CHAPTER 10:

SURRENDER AND RECEIVE PEACE

God has given us peace, but how do we truly receive this peace more abundantly? We must surrender and "totally submit to Him" (James 4:7-8, NKJV), allow Jesus to take over our lives completely, trust in Him, love Him, and hope in Him (Isaiah 26:3-4; Jeremiah 17:7-8; Proverbs 29:25). "Those who trust in the Lord, mercy shall surround him" (Psalm 32:10, NKJV).

Jesus said, "Peace I leave with you, My peace I give to you; not as the world gives do I give to you" (John 14:27, NKJV). Psalm 29:11 declares, "The Lord will bless His people with peace." "The Lord will truly put gladness in your heart, and you will lie down in peace and sleep" (Psalm 4:7-8). "The Lord will bless His people with peace"

(Psalm 29:11). The Lord will truly put gladness in your heart, and "you will lie down in peace and sleep" (Psalms 4:7-8).

I am a living witness because the Lord healed my broken heart, wiped away my tears with His love, and filled me with peace, courage, boldness, a merry heart, joy and gladness, and sweet sleep. I was totally transformed. The Lord will also help you to forgive everyone that has hurt you because it is impossible without Jesus, but things will surely get easier after one surrenders to the Lord. He will truly give you a new heart, a heart of flesh. God will remove the heart of stone out from you (Ezekiel 36:26-27) and bless you with an obedient heart, a heart to love Him more, a heart to praise Him more, a tender, loving, and caring heart towards others, a heart of compassion, patience, kindness, and forgiveness. He did it for me.

I have been an advocate for forgiveness since the Holy Spirit said in one of my meetings in Bangalore, India, "For I am one crying in the wilderness for forgiveness." The Lord is crying out because He knows the consequences of unforgiveness. Please give Him a chance to help you forgive. If one does not forgive, demons have the right to take possession and torment. The Lord wants to take control of our lives, character, and behavior, so will you be able to surrender totally to Him? Will you allow Him to take over your life? **Please permit Jesus to take the driver's seat in your life.** When one surrenders their heart to the Lord, He opens them apart and deep cleans; He removes the old man in you, the old man that is full of pride, lies, condescension, deceit, corruption, anger, unforgiveness, and much more, and He gives you the new man, a new creation (Ephesians 4:22-24, NKJV).

Apostle Paul tells us, "Even though our outward man is perishing, yet the inward man is being renewed day by day" (2 Corinthians 4:16, NKJV). The Spirit of God slowly transforms us to be Christ-like; things of the Kingdom are slow. As Christians, we must "be transformed by renewing of our mind" (Romans 12:1-2, NKJV). According to my professor at the university (Liberty Seminary), "He will make you a better you" (Dr. Robert Stacy) because the Lord made Amba a better Amba.

A scholar, Paul Pettit argues, "Change is not optional for the believer in Jesus Christ, the relationship should be continually growing, improving, and maturing. God is the one who enables and brings about the change." So please, "cling to Him" (Jeremiah 13:11). As Christians, we must be transformed; do not just be a church-goer, because part of Christianity is change in character: "We must trust the Lord with our future and improve" (Sister Faustina). Spiritual transformation is the things you love to do before accepting Christ but you must let go of them.

Apostle Paul affirms, "One thing I do, forgetting those things which are behind and reaching forward to those things which are ahead" (Philippians 3: 13-14, NKJV). Paul knew that God is our only source of salvation as well as the source of our spiritual growth. The closer we get to completion, the more we realize how much further we must go to become like Christ. So, be encouraged by Paul and Sister Faustina's emphasis here by forgetting the past and straining forward to what lies ahead you.

Our past mistakes, for example—what should have been done that was not accomplished: the failed marriages or relationships, children that were left behind because of failed relationships, the physical abuse, the many stripes on one's body, the broken forehead, loosed teeth that needed dental implants (which has formed gum disease), eye surgeries that were needed due to physical abuse, verbal abuse that pierces into one's heart, the hurt, disappointments, heart aches that have been tolerated, weeping in the presence of children, finances and possessions that were left behind or seized.

We all have a past that affects and controls our thoughts, but when this is the case, we miss God's blessings and purpose in our lives. Especially women as we get older, we tend to remember or recollect a lot that has happened in the past. So please let go because the Lord uses our miserable past for His glory, to encourage others through one's ministry.

What mankind calls a terrible experience, in God's eyes it is good, and He will not waste it. Although the Devil will want you to shut your mouth and be quiet about it, you will keep meditating on your past experiences. For example, what Susan and Caroline did to you almost forty years ago or what your grandfather said that he should not have said—please let go. The Devil will oppress you in a way that you will find it difficult to forgive or let go. Please ask Jesus to help you, because He too went through temptations, and He will surely aid in challenging times.

CHAPTER 11:

MY TESTIMONY ABOUT FORGIVENESS

I had a habit of not saying a word each time an individual offended me, but I would cry to the Lord. So, one fine day as I planned to weep after Church service, the Lord stopped me and said, "What are you doing? Did they nail you on the Cross? Did you carry the Cross for anyone?"

Please think about this for a moment; because of His comments, my attitude changed, and I now pray for the individuals. For my heart to be protected, I donned a vest given to me by the Lord.

Jesus is such a loving Father, so tenderhearted who loves His own. Jesus went through so much because of love. Please permit me to ask you the same question: "Did anyone nail you on the Cross? Did you carry the Cross for anyone?" The Lord is willing to help you forgive because unforgiveness opens doors for unclean spirits to dwell in you, which causes hindrances, sicknesses, hatred, depression, anger, and unhappiness.

During one of my meetings in India, the Lord said, "I am One crying in the wilderness for forgiveness." The Lord cried out. He is still crying out because of the great love He has towards us, His children. Letting go of the past, forgetting the past can sometimes be difficult, but we are required to let go and forgive so Christ can be exalted in us.

Please do not allow your past pain and suffering to control you; we should no longer be influenced by our past. God's grace will take us through the consequences of our past sins/mistakes. Apostle Paul is a perfect example of this truth, that we should not allow past grudges or bitterness to control us. "But one thing I do, forgetting what is behind and straining toward what is ahead, I press on toward the goal to win the prize for which God has called me heavenward in Christ Jesus" (Philippians 3:13-14, NIV).

Our Lord Jesus asked the Father to forgive those who nailed Him on the cross, "For they do not know what they do" (Luke 23:34, NKJV). How much more you and me? Love is a Kingdom policy. Apostle Paul tells us, "Be kind and compassionate to one another, forgiving each other just as in Christ, God forgave you" (Ephesians 4:32, NIV). And I have been commanded to be compassionate and patient towards others.

Jesus said, "Amba, say the Word with a command." Please pray with the Word because "the Word is like a hammer, like a fire" (Jeremiah 23:29). The Word runs very swiftly, and God will never say no to His Word. Prayer is you reading His Word back to Him, and always "[p]our out your heart before the Lord" (Psalm 62:8). He loves it. Not to a friend, sister, or your mother, but to the Lord, and put on your spiritual jacket which is praise and worship, while cooking or cleaning. It is your weapon.

I was set free from unforgiveness.

CHAPTER 12:

TRUST IN THE LORD

SCRIPTURE PASSAGES:

Shortly before I followed the Lord to Bangalore, India, He said, "Amba, you must trust Me, and you must be a member of My fire department." And I wondered why. But at about 2am, I was awakened by the Lord: "Get up and release fire, for the Devil has entered your room." With sleepy eyes, I tried to fall back to sleep, but the Lord insisted I get up and release fire on the Devil. Toothless Devil, he left in a speed. He is the God of great powers, and I placed my trust in Him right after that statement. Yes, God has a fire department in Heaven, and I am a member.

Scripture advises us to trust in the Lord, hope in Him, love Him, and wait patiently for Him, for His ways are different from our ways. In that waiting period, there will be deliverance, healing, and cleansing. He will also guide, teach, and mentor you.

TESTIMONY:

A brother who lived in Oman was wrongfully laid off from his place of work, and I was contacted to intercede. The Lord said, "Amba, trust in Me." I was also commanded to pay a vow on behalf of this brother using Psalms 50:14-15: "Offer to God thanksgiving and pay your vows to the Most High. Call upon Me in the day of trouble; I will deliver you, and you shall glorify Me." All the barriers were broken down, and his job was restored to him. Afterwards, I encouraged other brothers and sisters in the Lord to make a vow to the Lord in time of need. We must trust in the Lord.

Psalm 37:5 tells us, "Commit your way to the Lord; trust in Him and He will do it for you" (NIV). God is our Father; if one trusts an earthly father, why not your heavenly Father who is the Creator of all things, God of all flesh, who is our healer, provider, and deliverer?

"Be still and know that I am God. I will be

exalted among the nations, and I will be exalted in the earth!" (Psalm 46:10). Scripture tells us, "And whatever you ask in My name, that I will do, that the Father may be glorified in the Son. If you [a]sk anything in my name, I will do it" (John 14:13–14, NKJV). Please ask with a humble and sincere heart. "Do not be anxious about your life, what you will eat or what you will drink, nor about your body, what you will put on. Is life not more than food, and the body more than clothing?" (Matthew 6:25). The Lord has not forsaken those who put their trust in Him, because He is a faithful God. "And those who know Your name put their trust in You, for You, O Lord, have not forsaken those who seek You" (Psalm 9:10). "And we know that for those who love God all things work together for good, for those who are called according to His purpose" (Romans 8:28). When you trust in the Lord, do not be afraid, for He is with you. "You will not be afraid of bad news; for your heart is firm, trusting in the Lord" (Psalm 112:7).

We must be courageous and strong, for our Father is mighty in battle and a deliverer who makes a way where there is no way. "Have I not commanded you? Be strong and courageous, do not be frightened, and do not be dismayed, for the Lord your God is with you wherever you go" (Joshua 1:9). Omnipresent God who is in millions of places at the same time—Hallelujah! "Do not fear, only believe" (Mark 5:36). "God will keep you in perfect peace when you trust in Him" (Isaiah 26:3). God said in Jeremiah 33:3, "Call to Me, and I will answer you, and show you great and mighty things, which you do not know."

Brothers and sisters, please call on the Lord, pray to Him, trust in Him, read His Word back to Him, and wait. Do not fight your battles yourself; always pray and ask the Lord for help, because our battles belong to Him. Your enemies will be defeated before you. Hallelujah! But you must believe.

He is such a loving Father who is always there for us, His children. He said, "With His everlasting arms, He will thrust the enemies from before you and say! Destroy them!" (Deuteronomy 33:27). He will always do in accordance with His Word.

In 1 Samuel 7:5-13, Samuel trusted the Lord; for example, Samuel the prophet and the children of Israel were offering a burnt offering to the Lord, and the Philistines drew near for battle. Samuel cried out to the Lord for Israel, and the Lord answered his prayers. He thundered with a loud thunder upon the Philistines that day, and so confused them, and they were overcome before Israel. 2 Kings 18, 19:6-7 tells us, the King of Assyria troubled King Hezekiah of Judah, the King of Assyria even went as far as blaspheming God Almighty, so King Hezekiah tore his clothes and sent messages to prophet Isaiah. But God said, "Surely, I will send a spirit upon the King of Assyria, and he will hear a rumor and return to his land; and I will cause him to fall by the sword in his own land" (Isaiah 37:7). In verse 35, "The Angel of the Lord went out and killed in the camp of the Assyrians one hundred and eighty-five thousand; and when the people arose early in the morning there were the corpses—all dead." Verse 37 says, "The sons of the King of Assyria killed him while he was worshipping his useless idols."

The battle is the Lords; surrender to Him, for 2 Chronicles 20:1-23 affirms, "The people of Ammon, Moab, and Mount Seir came together to fight against Judah." So, the King of Judah called on the Lord; please notice that the King of Judah did not call his friends to complain; he did not call his parents, but he called on the Lord, and the Lord answered his prayers. Our Father fought the battles of the King of Judah, "for the people of Ammon and Moab stood up against the inhabitants of Mount Seir to utterly destroy them. And when they had put an end to the inhabitants of Mount Seir, they helped destroy one another."

Judah's enemies destroyed themselves, so Judah did not have to fight. The Lord fought their battles and defeated all their enemies. He will always fight your battles if you call to Him and put your trust in the Lord Most High. Allow Him to take the driver's seat in your life, you and your family.

CHAPTER 13:

HUMILITY

Most individuals are extremely deceitful, thinking it is wisdom. Jesus stepped down into this wicked wilderness we call home with total humility. He who is the Author of life, the Prince of life, the Originator of life was born in a room for animals, laid on a bed for animals, and wrapped with clothing for animals as planned. Without Jesus, the things that were created were never created, so who are we to be proud? To be condescending? OH wretched sinners that we are. I often talk about pride because God cannot go near those who are proud; we must be humble, for God kicked Satan out of His presence because of pride. Matthew 23:12 asserts, "Whoever exalts himself will be humbled."

Children of God, the Church of Christ, the

Assembly of God, the Unity of Christ, the heart of Jesus, must not be proud. For the Lord said, "The Church is My heart." What a touching statement. Jesus teaches about a parable of humility, which is dear to His heart because pride is sinful in the sight of God and is self-centered rather than God-centered. "When you are invited by anyone to a wedding feast, do not sit down in the best place lest one more honorable than you be invited by him; and he who invited you and him come and say to you, give place to this man, and then you begin with shame to take the lowest place. But when you are invited, go, and sit down in the lowest place, so that when he who invited you comes, he may say to you, friend, go up higher. Then you will have glory in the presence of those who sit at the table with you. For whoever exalts himself will be humbled, and he who humbles himself will be exalted" (Luke 14:8-11).

As part of mankind, when one is invited to an event, we tend to look for the best seats, which is pride. But the Lord is advising us to be humble, to choose the lowest seat or wait to be seated, for it is very shameful when one is asked to change seats to a much lower one; do not let yourselves to be exposed to shame.

Jesus indicates that "whoever humbles himself as these little children is the greatest in the kingdom of heaven" (Matthew 18:4). "Humble yourselves in the sight of the Lord, and He will lift you up" (James 4:10); Luke 14:11; 1 Peter 5:6). Proverbs 6:17 affirms, one of the six things that the Lord hates, is a proud look, and "God opposes the proud but gives grace to the humble" (James 4:6). Pride is sin, and, because God is Holy, He cannot withstand sin; His heart's desire is always to deliver us, to set us free from the evil ones.

Most pastors have allowed red carpets to be laid out for them, which is pride. Question: Were red carpets laid out for Jesus who came with total humility? Who walked from city to city, town to town, and village to village proclaiming the Good News? For it is written, "And being found in appearance as a man, He humbled Himself and became obedient to the point of death, even the death of the cross" (Philippians 2:8). Praise the Lord.

The story that comes to mind is the story of King Hezekiah who was very sick and at the point of death, so God sent Isaiah the prophet to the king and told him to put his house in order because he will die—surely die. King Hezekiah turned his face towards the wall and prayed and wept. The Bible tells us King Hezekiah wept bitterly, so God sent Isaiah back to Hezekiah and said He will heal him and deliver him from the king of Assyria; God added fifteen years onto his life. King Hezekiah then, had visitors from Babylon because they heard he was sick. What did King Hezekiah do? He showed off his wealth, everything he owned, such as gold, silver, precious ointments, and so on, but failed to glorify God for his healing (2 Kings 20:1–6).

Isaiah 39:1–8 also tells us, "Hezekiah should have glorified God for his healing but showed off his wealth to the Babylonians." "He did not repay according to the favor shown him; for his heart was lifted [pride]; therefore, wrath [anger] was looming over him and over Judah and Jerusalem" (2 Chronicles 32:25). Verse 26 of the same book says, "he humbled himself immediately."

Brothers and sisters, God values thanksgiving and gratitude. Pride is of the Devil; please seek to be delivered. "For whoever exalts himself will be humbled, and he who humbles himself will be exalted" (Matthew 23:12). "For before honor is humility" (Proverbs 18:12). Hallelujah! "What comes out of a person is what defiles him"—from your heart—pride (Mark 7:20-22). Please do not look down on people and talk down on people; embrace them and love them, for God is love.

The concluding part of this parable advises us that, "When you give a dinner or a supper, do not ask your friends, your brothers, your relatives, nor rich neighbors, lest they also invite you back, and you be repaid. But when you give a feast, invite the poor, the maimed, the lame, the blind. And you will be blessed, because they cannot repay you; for you shall be repaid at the resurrection of the just" (Luke 14:12-14).

If you cannot invite them to your home, please support them, for example with clothing, food, and sanitary items. For Deuteronomy 15:11 tells us, "The poor will never cease from the land; therefore, I command you, saying, you shall open your hand wide to your brother, to your poor and your needy, in your land." If you have two slices of bread, please give one slice to your neighbor, and the Lord will surely repay you.

HUMILITY CONTINUED:

Luke 18:9-14 tells us, two men went to the Temple to pray, one a Pharisee and the other a tax collector. In this parable, the Pharisee signifies a proud individual, who is a wealthy, wise, condescending, arrogant, rude, and deceitful individual; he is also greedy and a liar, for while praying, the Pharisee who is full of pride said, I am not like other men, extortioners [take something by force], unjust, adulterers [The Pharisee who probably has a mistress], or even like this tax collector."

The Pharisee said, "I fast and pay tithes," which is first class pride. When you look down on others, condescending and proud, your fasting and tithes will never be accepted. Please repent and humble yourselves because the Lord hates pride. For Scripture tells us, "But the poor humble man, in his humility, raised his eyes towards heaven, beat his breast saying, be merciful unto me a sinner" (Luke 18:13). He acknowledged his sins—total humility.

He said, please have mercy.

He wept.

And the Lord, in His mercy that is so rich and love that is great, answered the poor man's prayers. God hates pride, "A haughty look, and a proud heart" (Proverbs 21:4). "The one who has a haughty look and a proud heart, him I will not endure" (Psalm 101:5); and "[h]e who is greatest among you shall be your servant. And whoever exalts himself will be humbled, and he who humbles himself will be exalted" (Matthew 23:11-12).

TESTIMONY ABOUT HOW I SERVED A FAMILY AND DID IT WITH IMMENSE JOY:

I was once invited by a family for prayers; I also decided to help; for example, I swept their floors, washed their dishes, and took great care of their little children, but were they grateful? No, because of pride and arrogance; they were just condescending individuals. Because of their arrogance and ungratefulness, I wept to the Lord, but He said, "You are My servant." The Lord taught me to do good, to be kinder, even though some will never appreciate any kindness and goodness shown to them.

On another occasion, I was sent to a sister who was sick by the Lord (she had cancer and later passed on). The Lord asked me to buy a tray of Chinese rice for this sister and her family, but arriving at her home, I went straight to the kitchen, washed all the pots and pans, counter tops, hoovered and washed the floors and went with them to church for midweek prayers. They were a grateful family.

Please continue doing good,
and the Lord will repay you in time.

PROUD PASTORS:

The Lord asked me to start an online prayer, which I did, but He insisted, stressed on a "humble heart," which is extremely important to the Lord. He cannot work well with those who have a proud heart and a haughty look.

I once met a pastor in Canada who, while preaching, bragged about what he had on, for example, the many expensive cars for his 9 to 10 years old children, and his expensive shoes (worth 10,000 dollars).

Pastors who have allowed red carpets to be rolled out for them use the pulpit to abuse members of the Church. Please do not do such things; be careful because you will be humbled by the Lord, disgraced, and your tables turned upside-down. The Lord will put you down.

Paul also criticizes the rich in the Church at Corinth for humiliating the poor by failing to share their fine food with them. For Paul, the unity we share in Christ means all believers are equal in God's eyes and worthy of equal honor and respect (1 Corinthians 11:17-34). The First Century Roman sources even described guests being placed in different dining rooms in this grading of status; it was clearly the order of the day and reflected the values of this honor/shame culture. It is this kind of culture that lies behind Jesus' teaching in Luke 14: "Love all people."

Jesus Christ lives out of this concern for maintaining social status as He eats with tax collectors and sinners (Matthew 9:9-13; 11:19). Let us allow Jesus's footsteps to be our pathway, imitate Jesus, and be spiritually transformed to be Christ-like.

Please put on your spiritual jacket (**which is praise and worship**)

Praise is beautiful to the Lord. **Hallelujah!**

CHAPTER 14

DISOBEDIENCE

THE DOCTRINE OF SIN:

Most of our actions and behaviors are done out of ignorance, and we are disciplined by it without knowing we have sinned against the Living God who is Holy, intensely Holy.

SIN:

Jesus Himself explicitly claimed to be righteous; He asked His audience, "Can any of you prove Me guilty of sin?" (John 8:46); no one replied. He also maintained, "I always do what pleases the Father Who sent Me" (John 8:29). Again, "I have kept My Father's commandments" (John 15:10). He taught His disciples to confess their sins and ask for forgiveness, but there is no report of Jesus confessing sins and asking forgiveness on His own behalf.

TESTIMONY:

I never knew disobedience is sin, although sometimes they are done out of ignorance, and ignoring the voice of the Lord is also sinful. All of these I do frequently and get disciplined often by the Lord, so when I started my studies, (Master of Arts in Theological Studies) I spent more time studying out of ignorance, and I was frequently disciplined for spending too much time studying rather than being in the Lord's presence.

My middle finger was bent and painful; I had frequent boils, painful lips, painful ankle, painful knees, painful back and waist, dizziness, weakness, and much more. But as soon as I decided to study for two hours each day, I was completely healed. The Lord wanted me to spend more time with Him, and I did not know it; I now pray frequently during the day and read at least four chapters of the Bible daily.

I have also learned to repent immediately whenever I realize my wrong, getting down on my knees, praying, and weeping to the Lord and asking for forgiveness. I also fast three days each month, interceding for the Church (the body of Christ), the Nations, those who are sick, and my family. As a servant of God, it is important for me to be obedient to the Lord, for He is intensely Holy (Holy, Holy, Holy Majesty). It is also important that mankind listen when God speaks, because disobedience follows upon failure to hear correctly. It might sometimes take a few prayers, weeping and fasting, but it is worth it. His name is "God-Who-Forgives" (Psalm 99:8). What a Loving Father.

- God expects obedience (Deuteronomy 11:26-28).
- To choose Christ is to choose obedience (John 14:15,21).
- To become disobedient is to sin or rebel against God (I Samuel 15:22,23).

WHAT IS SIN?

Godwin Wenham affirms, "Augustine's starting point was the perfection of the first man Adam before he fell. (Firstly) All sinned in Adam. (Secondly) the fall results in the corruption of human nature, so everyone now falls far short of the moral and physical perfection that Adam enjoyed. Man is enslaved to ignorance, to a godless search for pleasure and to death. Moral struggle and failure are the fruit of the fall and an aspect of original sin. (Thirdly) original sin deprives us of free will, so that we cannot avoid sin without God's help."

According to J.B. Pratt, "God is righteousness Himself; that which He does is right and that is right which He does. Obedience to His will, moreover, is the criterion of right for all His creatures. But Augustine does not stop here as so many theologians do. He adds, "It is our duty to do the will of God because His will is our deepest will too."

Consider the words of King David in Psalm 51:4: "Against You, You only, have I sinned and done what is evil in Your sight" (NIV).

The words of D.A. Carson here are helpful: "At one level, of course, this is blatantly untrue: David has sinned against Bathsheba, her husband, her child, his family, military high command, and the nation, which he serves as chief magistrate. Yet there is something profound in David's words, what makes sin, sin in the deepest sense, is that it is against God. What makes them worthy of punishment by God Himself, is that they are first, foremost, and most deeply sins against the Living God, who has made us for Himself and to whom we must one day give an account." So, what is sin? According to George Zemek, sin is "[a]ny personal lack of conformity to the moral character or desire of God." Zemek lists the dimensions of sin as follows:

(1) Sin: a disposition of the heart (for example, a state).
(2) Sin: a thought (for example, an impulse, intent), (Matt. 5:27-28).
(3) Sin: an act.
(4) Sin: an omission (Leviticus 5:17-19; James 4:17). For us, "the sequence of sin begins with nature and proceeds with thought then action or omission. With Adam the thought preceded the nature."

According to Augustine's definition of sin, the order of concept, "sin is disorder."

"Original sin was an expression of disorder which implanted disorder in the very core of human nature." Luther also indorsed this line. Regarding sin, Apostle Paul tells us, "For what I am doing, I do not understand, for what I will to do, that I do not practice; but what I hate, that I do. If then, I do what I will not do, I agree with the law is good. But now, it is no longer I who do it, but sin that dwells in me. For I know that in me (that is, in my flesh) nothing good dwells; for to will is present with me, but how to perform what is good I do not find. For the good that I will do, I do not do; but the evil I will not do, that I practice, now if I do what I will not to do, it is no longer I who do it, but sin that dwells in me" (Romans 7:15-20, NKJV).

In Christian views, sin is an evil act which violates God's nature. Sin is an act of offence against God by ignoring His laws. 1 John 3:4 tells us, "Everyone who sins breaks the law; in fact, sin is lawlessness" (NIV). "See, I set before you today life and prosperity, death, and destruction. For I command you today to love the Lord your God, to walk in obedience to Him, and to keep His commands, decrees, and laws; then you will live and increase, and the Lord your God will bless you in the land you are entering to possess" (Deuteronomy 30:15-16, NIV). "Love the Lord

your God with all your heart and with all your soul and with all your mind and love your neighbor as yourself" (Matthew 22:35-40, NIV). "This is love for God, to keep His commands, and His commands are not burdensome" (1 John 5:3, NIV).

Sin is also violation of the law of love; as mankind, we must be obedient to the Lord and love one another as Christ loves us. Be caring towards each other? Wash one another's feet? Forgive each other? This is love. God has shown us the way in which we must live, but mankind has turned the other way, the way to sin, the cares of the world. 1 John 5: 17 tells us, "All wrongdoing is sin" (NIV). Mankind needs to know that "calling individuals fool, murder and anger is also sin" (Matthew 5:21:22, NIV).

TESTIMONY OF TRANSFORMATION:

A few years ago, I wore so much gold; for example, double rings on each finger, double necklaces, and bracelets. Before stepping out of the house, it was as though my joy and beauty came from wearing this abundance of gold. The Lord took all of that away from me. I later came to realize that it was idolatry; thus, I was transformed by the Lord. The Scripture tells us, "Do not let your adornment be merely outward, arranging the hair, wearing gold, or putting on fine apparel, rather let it be the hidden person of the heart, with the incorruptible beauty of a gentle and quiet spirit, which is very precious in the sight of God" (I Peter 3:3-4, NKJV).

The core of sin is also unbelief; this has firm biblical support: In Genesis 3, Adam and Eve trusted the word of the serpent over the word of God; Scripture tells us Jesus Christ was rejected by the leaders of the Jews; in Acts 7, Stephen was martyred at the hands of unbelievers; and in John 20:24-25, Thomas arrogantly dismisses the resurrection of Jesus. Please pay more attention, brothers and sisters, because it is frightening to fall into the Hands of the Living God, so my prayer is to be extra careful, understand His commands, and act on His Word and commandments. Please also feel free to ask questions where you are not sure; our loving Father is always willing to explain. We must also know what the Lord is telling us and act accordingly. The key word is obedient.

SUS, TAKE THE DRIVER'S SEAT

JESUS, TAKE THE DRIVER'S SEAT

JESUS, TAKE THE DRIVER'S SEAT

"The acts of the flesh are obvious: sexual immorality, impurity, idolatry, and witchcraft; hatred, discord [strife among individuals], jealousy, fits of rage [anger], selfish ambition, dissensions, factions, and envy; drunkenness, orgies, and the like. I warn you, as I did before, that those who live like this will not inherit the kingdom of God"

GALATIANS 5:19-21

"If we claim to be without sin, we deceive ourselves and the truth is not in us, but if we confess our sins, He is faithful and just and will forgive us our sins and purify us from all unrighteousness. If we claim we have not sinned, we make Him out to be a liar and His word is not in us"

1 JOHN 1:8-10

"For we know that our old self was crucified with Jesus so that the body ruled by sin might be done away with, that we should no longer be slaves to sin"

ROMANS 6:6

"The Spirit of God came on Zechariah the son of Jehoiada the priest; and he stood above the people, and said to them, 'Thus says God, why do you disobey the commandments of the Lord, so that you cannot prosper? Because you have forsaken the Lord, He has also forsaken you'"

2 CHRONICLES 24:20

"I will purge out from among you the rebels, and those who disobey against me"

EZEKIEL 20:28

"One who believes in the Son has eternal life, but one who disobeys the Son will not see life, but the wrath of God remains on him"

JOHN 3:36

"Moses said, 'Why now do you disobey the commandment of the Lord, since it shall not prosper?'"

NUMBERS 14:41

"Who, then, are those who fear the Lord? He will instruct them in the ways they should choose"

PSALM 25:12, NIV

"The Lord confides in those who fear Him; He makes his covenant known to them"

PSALM 25:14, NIV

"Then the Church throughout Judea, Galilee and Samaria enjoyed a time of peace and was strengthened. Living in the fear of the Lord and encouraged by the Holy Spirit, it increased in numbers"

ACTS 9:31, NIV

God told Moses, "Take the rod; you and your brother Aaron, gather the congregation together. **Speak** [bold added for emphasis] to the rock before their eyes, and it will yield its water; thus, you shall bring water for them out of the rock, and give drink to the congregation and their animals" (Numbers 20: 8-12). **In verse11:** "Moses lifted his hand and **struck** [bold added for emphasis] the rock twice with his rod; and water came out abundantly, and the congregation and their animals drank." He disobeyed the Father, but God in His mercy that is rich still gave them water to drink. **But in verse 12,** God was angry with Moses and Aaron: "Then the Lord spoke to Moses and Aaron, because you did not **believe** [bold added for emphasis] Me, to hallow Me in the eyes of the children of Israel, therefore you shall not bring this assembly into the land which I have given them."

Moses and Aaron died not crossing over to the promised land—**the price of disobedience.**

SAUL'S DISOBEDIENCE:

"Samuel told Saul; The Lord sent me to anoint you king over His people Israel. Now therefore, heed the voice of the words of the Lord. Thus, says the Lord of Hosts: I will punish Amalek for what he did to Israel, how he ambushed him on the way when Israel came up from Egypt. Now go and attack Amalek and utterly destroy all that they have; do not spare them, but kill both man and woman, child and infant, ox and sheep, camel, and donkey" (1 Samuel 15:1-3).

Verse 9 says, "Saul and the people spared Agag and the best of the sheep, the oxen, the fatlings, the lambs, and all that was good, and were unwilling to utterly destroy them." **Saul's disobedience cost him his Kingship.**

KING SOLOMON ALSO FAILED AS A KING:

Scripture tells us, the king must not acquire a great number of horses (because the battle is the Lords). He must not take too many wives, because his heart will be led astray. He must not accumulate large number of silver and gold (Deuteronomy 17:14-17). Solomon's wives led him away from God with their idols. He said, "If you listen carefully to the Lord your God and do what is right in His eyes, if you pay attention to His commands and keep all His decrees, I will not bring on you any of the diseases I brought on the Egyptians, for I am the Lord, who heals you" (Exodus 15:26, NIV).

CHAPTER 15:

THE LORD WANTS TO TAKE THE DRIVER'S SEAT IN OUR LIVES

TESTIMONY:

I thought to pray deliverance prayers with the Word of God; for several years I did just that. For example, Jeremiah 30:23 tells us, "Behold the whirlwind of the Lord goes forth with furry, a continuing whirlwind. It will fall violently on the head of the wicked" (NKJV). Regarding the enemies, "Let them be like chaff before the wind, and let the angel of the Lord chase them. Let their way be dark and slippery, and let the angel of the Lord pursue them" (Psalm 35:5-6, NKJV).

"I will send My fear before you, I will cause confusion among all the people to whom you come and will make all your enemies turn their backs to you. And I will send hornets before you, which shall drive out the Hivite, the Canaanite, and the Hittite from before you" (Exodus 23:27-28, NKJV).

MY PRAYER:

Lord, I pray in accordance with Your Word in Jeremiah 30:23, let the whirlwind of the Lord fall upon the heads of all my enemies and enemies of my children in the mighty name of Jesus Christ. Do not spare them, Lord; send forth a very violent whirlwind and destroy my enemies, Lord, I pray in the mighty name of Jesus Christ. Father, Your Word says, "Call to Me, and I will answer you, and show you great and mighty things, which you do not know" (Jeremiah 33:3, NKJV).

Lord Jesus, show me great and mighty things, for I do not know anything; set us free, Lord, I pray, for Matthew 18:18 tells us, "Assuredly, I say to you, whatever you bind on earth will be bound in heaven, and whatever you loose on earth will be loosed in heaven" (NKJV).

TESTIMONIES:

As an intercessor, I used these Words to pray for individuals, binding and loosing. For it is written, "And I will give you the keys of the kingdom of heaven, and whatever you bind on earth will be bound in heaven, and whatever you loose on earth will be loosed in heaven" (Matthew 16:19, NKJV). Because of the way prayers were conducted, I suffered several attacks from the enemies of individuals I prayed for, so the Lord stopped me from praying that way. For example, I prayed for a sister who suddenly developed an itchy skin for about four days, and sleep was also taken from her.

After prayers, the Lord instantly healed her, but I developed an itchy skin. The Lord revealed to me many pits (like water wells). He sealed on my behalf that which the enemies had dug and continued to dig in order to destroy me. I once ran away from a car containing a coffin, which was meant for my burial, and from an invisible prison or detention center. I prayed for another sister once, and I was pursued in my dreams by a lady (probably a witch).

An elderly man entered my home in the middle of the night searching for me because I prayed for a sister using words that later the Lord stopped me from saying. And much more—the Lord is an excellent Teacher and Deliverer.

Beautiful deliverance prayers I thought were powerful, but the Lord suddenly changed my way of prayers to a simple and more powerful way of praying for individuals. It is for my protection (what a manner of love). As an intercessor (one who prays for others), the Lord decided to teach me other ways to pray, in order to stop the evil spirits and witches from attacking me in return.

Jesus said, allow Me to "take the driver's seat" in your live. For example, He fought all Israel's battles, and He is ready to fight ours also—so sweet.

Please allow the Lord to take the driver's seat in whatever area of difficulty you are going through (and mention the areas).

Some Scripture Verses that Tell us How God Fought Israel's Battles: (God took the driver's seat in their lives)

He sent them a prophet, who said, "This is what the Lord, the God of Israel, says: I brought you up out of Egypt, out of the land of slavery. I rescued you from the hand of the Egyptians. And I delivered you from the hand of all your oppressors; I drove them out before you and gave you, their land" (Judges 6:8-9, NKJV).

Israel's deliverance in Exodus 14 shows—what a Mighty God!

THE ANGEL AND THE PROMISES:

For it is written, "Behold, I send an Angel before you to keep you in the way and to bring you into the place which I have prepared. Beware of Him and obey His voice; do not provoke Him, for He will not pardon your transgressions; for My name is in Him. But if you indeed obey His voice and do all that I speak, then I will be an enemy to your enemies and an adversary to your adversaries. For My Angel will go before you and bring you in to the Amorites and the Hittites and the Perizzites and the Canaanites and the Hivites and the Jebusites; and I will cut them off" (Exodus 23:20-23, NKJV).

And Moses said to the people, "Do not be

afraid. Stand still, and see the salvation of the Lord, which He will accomplish for you today. For the Egyptians whom you see today, you shall see again no more forever, the Lord will fight for you, and you shall hold your peace" (Exodus 14:13-14, NKJV). "I will send My fear before you, I will cause confusion among all the people to whom you come and will make all your enemies turn their backs to you. And I will send hornets before you, which shall drive out the Hivite, the Canaanite, and the Hittite from before you. I will not drive them out from before you in one year, lest the land become desolate, and the beasts of the field become too numerous for you. Little by little I will drive them out from before you, until you have increased, and you inherit the land" (Exodus 23:27-30, NKJV).

"The Lord your God, who goes before you, He will fight for you, according to all He did for you in Egypt before your eyes" (Deuteronomy 1:30, NKJV). "When you go out to battle against your enemies and see horses and chariots and people more numerous than you, do not be afraid of them; for the Lord your God is with you, who brought you up from the land of Egypt. So it shall be, when you are on the verge of battle, that the priest shall approach and speak to the people. And he shall say to them, Hear, O Israel: Today you are on the verge of battle with your enemies. Do not let your heart faint, do not be afraid, and do not tremble or be terrified because of them; for the Lord your God is He who goes with you, to fight for you against your enemies, to save you" (Deuteronomy 20:1-4, NKJV). "So, the sun stood still, and the moon stopped, till the people had revenge upon their enemies. So, the sun stood still in the midst of heaven, and did not hasten to go down for about a whole day. And there has been no day like that, before it or after it, that the Lord heeded the voice of a man; for the Lord fought for Israel" (Joshua 10:13-14, NKJV). "And when he had consulted with the people, he appointed those who should sing to the Lord, and who should praise the beauty of holiness, as they went out before the army and were saying:

Praise the Lord,
For His mercy endures forever.

Now when they began to sing and to praise, the Lord set ambushes against the people of Ammon, Moab, and Mount Seir, who had come against Judah; and they were defeated. For the people of Ammon and Moab stood up against the inhabitants of Mount Seir to utterly kill and destroy them. And when they had made an end of the inhabitants of Seir, they helped to destroy one another. So, when Judah came to a place overlooking the wilderness, they looked toward the multitude; and there were their dead bodies, fallen on the earth. No one had escaped" (2 Chronicles 20:21-24, NKJV).

CHAPTER 16

FOCUS ON JESUS

STORMS:

Storms are part of life in this wicked evil wilderness we call home, so in times of storms, I always focus on Jesus, fix my eyes on Him, and stay in much prayer. For storms will surely come, but we must take courage and not lose hope.

For example, in the Gospel of Matthew, the 14th chapter, Jesus tells His disciples, "Take courage, for it is I, do not be afraid." Jesus was walking on water in the middle of the storm, and when His disciples saw Him, they were afraid because they thought He was a ghost. The disciples wondered what the purpose of the storm was, but Jesus' words demonstrate the purpose of the storm is to strengthen the disciples (to build courage and help them not feel fear at any time). But as mankind, we wonder how the disciples felt hearing the voice of Jesus in the middle of the storm and seeing Him walking on water—all fear was gone.

Elijah also struggled to hear God's voice amid being persecuted. It was only when he spent "the calm holy hour" in the cave that he was able to hear God's voice in the whisper. His quiet time in the cave helped him to identify God's voice. Also, the disciples' time with Jesus, "their years of training," helped them separate Jesus' voice from other voices.

Jesus commanded Peter to walk on water, and Peter did, but as Peter took his focus off Jesus and looked at the waves of the sea, fear gripped him, and he began to sink. The hands of Jesus are stretched out towards you and me; will you be able to take hold of His hands? Our Precious Savior.

I have learned to always fix my eyes on Jesus and not doubt, for God says when we focus on Him and acknowledge Him, He will deliver us. "Because he loves Me," says the Lord, "I will rescue him; I will protect him, for he acknowledges My name. He will call on Me, and I will answer him; I will be with him in trouble, I will deliver him and honor him." (Psalm 91:14-15) (NIV). What a great promise. The Lord will do as He has said, because of His faithfulness; He will protect and deliver you. We are required to "[fix] our eyes on Jesus, the pioneer and perfecter of faith" (Hebrews 12:1-2, NIV). Brothers and sisters, the moment our focus is off Jesus, we will go astray and begin to sink because of Satan and his agents. Romans 8:5 says, "Those who live according to the flesh have their minds set on what the flesh desires; but those who live in accordance with the Spirit have their minds set on what the Spirit desires."

The world is changing with more wickedness, evil desires, and much more, but God remains the same. His Word remains the same. Yes, God looks at the heart, so He said, "Amba, have a more compassionate heart, a heart of humility; love and be more patient with mankind." For He says, "You will seek Me and find Me when you seek Me with all your heart" (Jeremiah 29:13, NIV). We must also let go of the old man, the old man that is corrupt, full of lies and deceit, and put on the new man that is Christ-like and be transformed daily into the new man and focus on our Lord (Ephesians 4:22-24; John 6:63; Romans 8:9; 2 Corinthians 5:17, NKJV). **For Christianity is change.**

The key is prayer. The Lord commanded me to pray more, and I have, as the Lord commanded. A dear brother advised me to increase the temperature of my prayer to 100% degrees; I did, so something shifted. It is wonderful. Our Lord is loving and faithful. Apostle Matthew tells us, "Jesus prayed till dawn" (14:23-24). Most things will not come to us easily without many prayers, and that is because of enemies, known and unknown. **Amen!**

JESUS, TAKE THE DRIVER'S SEAT

CHAPTER 17

GENERATIONAL CURSE AND LIES

EXPLANATION:

Generational curses can be broken if only one trusts in the Lord Jesus and has faith in Him and His finished work on the Cross.

TESTIMONY:

My husband's father moved from city to city with his family while they were growing up, though, I learnt, it was due to work. My husband, I, and our children did the same, we moved from country to country, city to city, due to my husband's job but mainly because of the evil ones. We moved from England to California in 1996; in 2001 moved back to England; in 2002 moved back to California; in 2006 to Kitchener, Ontario, Canada; in 2009 back to California; in 2011 to Shamburg, Illinois; in 2014 to Surrey, British Columbia, Canada; and in 2017 to Austin, Texas. In every city, we tended to start all over because of the cost of shipping (the Devil's way of stealing finances). **It was a curse.**

My husband had a son before we met; he is now doing the same thing with his family, moving from country to country. My husband is verbally abusive; his son is also verbally abusive to his wife, friends, and family. My late father loved to drink alcohol, so his daughters followed suit, but the sons escaped that curse. To God be the glory because I was delivered in 2001 from alcohol. Alcohol is demonic, darkness, and it is Satan's territory.

We were once far off in darkness, in blindness, and in deceit covered with Satan's blanket of lies, "but in Christ Jesus we who were once far off have been brought near because of the blood of Jesus"—we are set free (Ephesians 2:13). "Jesus called us out of darkness into His marvelous light" (1 Peter 2:9-10).

Jesus said, "Amba, you are no longer in Satan's territory; you belong to Me, and I have bought you back with My shed blood on the Cross." At a "High Price" (1 Corinthians 6:20 and 1 Corinthians 7:23), we are His responsibility, and "He has also delivered us from the powers of darkness and conveyed us into the kingdom of the Son of His Love" (Colossians 1:13). We must claim it daily.

Most families in Africa, Canada, United States, India, and around the world suffer from generational curses. In most cases, all the women in a particular family will not get married or are divorced.

Most fathers who molest their daughters have sons who also molest their daughters. Fathers always get drunk or drink too much, and the children also drink too much alcohol. Fathers are abusive to their wives (verbal and physical abuse), the sons do the same. Fathers cheat on their wives, and most sons do the same. Parents that are proud, liars, condescending, and arrogant, have children who follow suit. These are all spirits.

SPIRITS OF INFIRMITIES THAT ARE GENERATIONAL:

Generational curses, spells, or spirits can be broken or disarmed because of the finished work of Jesus Christ on the Cross; for example, Galatians 3:13-14 tells us, "Christ redeemed us from the curse of the law by becoming a curse for us, for it is written; Cursed is everyone who is hung on a pole. He redeemed us in order that the blessings given to Abraham might come to the Gentiles through Christ Jesus, so that by faith we might receive the promise of the Spirit" (NIV). And Jesus has done it all on the Cross of Calvary; He took all our curses in His own body on the Tree. We must pray and declare it, pray for deliverance to be set free. For Colossians 2:15 also says, "And having disarmed the powers and authorities, he made a public spectacle of them, triumphing over them by the cross" (NIV).

Jesus has disarmed, demolished, destroyed, diffused, canceled, made of no more effect, scattered the powers of every evil spirit, powers of witches in our lives. Praise the Lord! The Bible did not promise us a life without suffering; we will, but it is not permanent, for Scripture says, "After you have suffered a while [God will] perfect, establish, strengthen and settle you" (1 Peter 5:10). His Word never goes void, but we must keep knocking, asking, and seeking (Matthew 7:7). And prayer is you reading His Word back to Him (and waiting on the Lord). He will surely take over your battles.

I love the story of the blind Bartimaeus in Mark 10:46–52: "When he heard that it was Jesus of Nazareth, he began to shout, 'Jesus, Son of David, have mercy on me!'" Brothers and sisters, we can do the same. Jesus, Son of the Most High God, have mercy on me, my family, and the whole world! We must call on Him until He stops, turns around, and asks, "What can I do for you?"

Jeremiah 13:11 says, "cling on to the Lord." Please do not let go.

CHAPTER 18

THE PROBLEM OF EVIL AND DEFENSE

EVIL:

God is perfect and has created a world that is perfect but gave mankind free will, and free will enables mankind to differentiate what is good and evil. As individuals, we are to follow the right path because the world we live in is full of evil, wickedness, and temptations. But some have gone the wrong way in the exercise of this freedom; this is the source of moral evil.

McFarland (a scholar), defined evil as "[s]omething which is against the good" (that which is against the will of God). Arthur M. affirms, "To appreciate the power of good, man needs to undergo the suffering caused by evil. It builds character and makes one strong such that he or she may face the hardships of life courageously" (p.128). Mankind is free to make moral choices, but sometimes these choices are evil and cause suffering, pain, sorrow, anger, rejections, hate, and death. Mankind can choose to obey God's commandments for peace and joy.

A scholar, Alvin Plantinga suggests, "God did in fact create significantly free creatures; but some of them went wrong in the exercise of freedom; this is the source of moral evil." Yes, God has given mankind free will because of His love that is so great, so intense, but it is up to mankind to use this free will to love our neighbors as ourselves—the commandment from Jesus—to help those in need, the poor, the homeless, to visit widows and the orphans, not to do evil and not to hurt or kill others. For example, if there is gun control in the United States, there will be less problem of evil; manufacturers of guns turned the other way because of wealth. If there is love in the hearts of most individuals, the problem of evil will surely be limited because love also covers a multitude of sins. Apostle Peter tells us, "Above all things, have a fervent love for one another, for love will cover a multitude of sins" (1 Peter 4:8). And Apostle Paul declares, "love is the end of the law" (Romans 13:8). If mankind can love one another the way God loves us, then there will be no mass shootings, theft, or much more.

Are we able to do good and seek God? Yes, because a few years ago, Uganda, a country in Africa, suffered famine, hunger, drought, and diseases such as Aids. So, an election took place, and the country elected a Christian president who called for a national three days of fasting and prayer; the people in Uganda showed up in their National Stadium, fasted, and prayed, using the Scripture 2 Chronicles 7:14—"If My people who are called by My name will humble themselves, pray and seek My face, and turn from their wicked ways, then I will hear from heaven, and will forgive their sins and heal their land" (NKJV). God healed and restored their land; Aids disappeared. The Lord turned the country of Uganda around, and the country flourished and prospered. "The Lord is slow to anger, abounding in love and forgiving sins and rebellion" (Numbers 14:18, NIV). If only mankind will seek Him and pray, God will surely forgive and restore.

> St. Hippo Augustine argues,
> "The solution of evil is
> to do the right thing."

In most nations on this planet earth, individuals have blindly gone the wrong way, choosing evil in place of good, choosing to worship idols in place of worshiping God, choosing to kill or hurt neighbors in place of loving them. Evil exists by man falling away from God and good, thus bringing about the corruption of mankind. For example, in the United States, there were mass shootings in an Elementary School in Uvalde, Texas, mass shooting in the grocery store at Buffalo, New York, church shooting in California, and Church shooting in Lagos, Nigeria, where Muslim extremist entered a Catholic church during service and left a bomb to explode, but as the Christians ran out of the church, shots were fired at them, killing about fifty people instantly. Evil has no purpose except to turn mankind away from pursuing good, but God is very merciful and compassionate. His heart's desire is for us to seek Him, pray to Him, praise Him, love Him, and acknowledge that He is our Father.

A scholar, B. Kyle Keltz, adds, "God is loving because His Will is for the good of His children at every moment they exist and guide them to Himself."

OH! What a manner of love.

Without Jesus, the flesh is weak, so the Scripture advises us to "[p]ut on the Lord Jesus Christ and make no provision for the flesh to fulfill its lust" (Romans 13:14). Kill this flesh, brothers and sisters, let the old man go and let the new man come. Spiritual transformation. Be renewed in the spirit (Ephesians 4:22-24). We must be transformed to be Christ-like, for again I say, Christianity is change.

A scholar, Ian A. McFarland, suggests, "God's attitude towards evil is always to condemn it." Which was what He did on the Cross: condemned evil, demolished and destroyed their powers. Satan's plans are now declared null and void.

Alvin Plantinga adds, "The heart of the Free-Will defense is a claim which is possible that God could have created a universe containing moral good and moral evil. And if so, then it is possible that God has a good reason for creating a world containing evil." Isaiah 45:7 says, "I form the light, and create darkness: I make peace, and create evil: I the Lord do all these things." Genesis 4:7 declares, "If you do not do well, sin lies at the door, and it's desire is for you, but you should rule over it." How? We shall rule over sin by repentance and asking for forgiveness. Our most loving Father is always willing to forgive us of all our sins and cleanse us of all unrighteousness. Yes, God sometimes likes to display His Mighty Powers so mankind will truly know who He is and what He can do.

The Scripture that comes to mind is the book of Exodus where God said, "For this purpose I have raised you up, that I may show My power in you, and that My name may be declared in all the earth" (Exodus 9:16). Up until then, the Gentiles did not know there was One True Living God, One God, the Creator, that through Him all things were created and His powers are limitless. Again, **by revelation**, the Lord said, "I created Moses for that very purpose," to lead the Israelites out of Egypt. Praise the Lord!

CHRISTIANS BELIEVE:

Jesus took all our sins in His own body on the Cross, but we must believe. For it is written, "The one who lies is of the devil, for the devil has lied from the beginning, for this purpose the Son of God was made manifest that He might destroy the works of the devil" (1 John 3:8). Praise the Lord! "He has delivered us from the powers of darkness and has conveyed us into the kingdom of the Son of His love, Jesus Christ"; we are with Jesus in His Kingdom (Colossians 1:13, NKJV). He has also "[d]isarmed principalities and powers, and made a public spectacle of them, triumphing over them in it, the Cross" (Colossians 2:15, NKJV).

The Parable of the Wheat and Tares tells us, "He who sows the good seed is the Son of Man, the field is the world, the good seeds are the sons of the kingdom, but the tares are the sons of the wicked one. The enemy who sowed them is the devil, the harvest is the end of the age, and the reapers are the angels. Therefore, as the tares are gathered and burned in the fire, it will be at the end of this age. The Son of Man will send out His angels, and they will gather out of His kingdom all those that offend, and those who practice lawlessness will be cast into the furnace of fire. There will be wailing and gnashing of teeth. Then the righteous will shine forth as the sun in the kingdom of their Father" (Matthew 13:36-43). Will you be one of those? Please accept Jesus Christ as your personal Lord and Savior.

God will finally rectify (put right, correct) evil when He judges the world, ushering into His eternal kingdom those persons who have been saved through Christ and sending to eternal hell those persons who are wicked and disobedient. So, currently, God is working to bring those whom He has chosen into His Kingdom where there is bright light, order, discipline, love, peace, joy, unity, oneness, compassion, and forgiveness. Jesus will return with great power and glory, casting every evil into the lake of fire on the final judgment day.

The heavens and earth will also be renewed. What a joy that day will be! All mankind will live in peace, unity, and harmony forever, but we must believe and let go of the old man in us and allow the new man to come with total change.

Brothers and sisters, why are we still slaves to sin? Why do we still lie; why do we still hate our brothers and sisters? Why do we still have jealous feelings? Anger, pride, deceit, condescending ways, evil thoughts? Evil desires? And lust? Please let the old man be crucified and follow Jesus to the cross in total surrender.

Galatians 5:16 tells us, "Walk in the Spirit, and you shall not fulfill the lust of the flesh." Please walk in the Spirit to quench the lust of the flesh and focus on Jesus. "You are a new creation; old things have passed away; behold all things have become new" (2 Corinthians 5:17). Please let the new man come.

- Have you been able to let go of pride?
- Have you been able to let go of verbal abuse? Physical abuse?
- Lies? Condescending ways? Gossiping? Anger?

We must die to our own ambitions, dreams, and desires, and allow Jesus to take over, for He is the Door and the Way; He knows what is best for you and me, because it takes place in the spiritual realm—spiritual transformation. Spiritually, we must offer the old man to be crucified; then we will no longer be slaves to sin. We must allow the Lord to "[o]pen our eyes and turn from darkness to light, and from the power of Satan to God, so that we may receive forgiveness of sins and a place among those who are sanctified by faith in God" (Acts 26:18, NIV).

Brothers and sisters, "We are a chosen people, a royal priesthood, a holy nation, God's special possession, that you may declare the praises of Him who called us out of darkness into His wonderful light" (1 Peter 2:9, NIV). We are a priced possession of the Lord, much loved, God's beloved children, so we must act as children of the Most High God.

Please learn how to swim in His love, intense love.

A new sin-free life, daily surrendering to the Lord, will definitely help mankind. I am not saying it is easy, but the Holy Spirit will help us if we only ask. Brothers and sisters, the way to Heaven is very narrow, but the way to Hell is extremely broad. Please take the narrow way and cling onto Jesus. The broad way is very sweet, drunken, womanizing, but by the time one realizes, it will be too late. Hell is very dark and smelly; please avoid going there.

Pour your heart to Him,
for He is our loving Father.

CHAPTER 19

CHRISTOLOGY/ THE MIRACLES OF JESUS CHRIST

PART OF CHRISTOLOGY IS THE STUDY OF JESUS, THE SON OF GOD:

Our Lord Jesus Christ has great powers over all things in this world we call home. For example, He has authority over people (Matthew 4:20,22). Peter and Andrew, his brother, left their net and followed Jesus; James and John his brother, sons of Zebedee, also left their father and followed Jesus.

For it is written,

- Jesus has power over the paralysis and suffering (Matthew 6:8,13; Luke 13:10-13).
- He has power over illnesses and diseases (Matthew 9:22; 14:35,36).
- He has power over blindness (Matthew 9:30; Mark 8:22-26).

- Jesus has power over leprosy (Mark 1: 40-45; Matthew 8:3).
- He has power over the wind and the water (Matthew 8:23-27; Luke 8:24).
- Jesus has power over the Temple (Matthew 12:3-6).
- Jesus has power over sin (Matthew 9:2).
- He has great power over demons (Mark 5:1-20; Matthew 8:31-32; 15:28; Luke 11:14; Luke 8:26-39).
- He has power over Nature (Matthew 21:18-19).
- Jesus has power over history (Matthew 26:64).
- Jesus has power over His own destiny (Matthew 16:21).
- He has great power over His mission on earth (Matthew 10:1).
- Jesus has great power over the dead (Luke 8:40-56; Luke 7:11-18).
- He has power over space, time, and the future (Matthew 18:19-20;28:20).

Our Lord Jesus started His ministry with healing and deliverance; for example, He entered a Synagogue and met a man of an unclean spirit. Luke tells us, "The spirit cried out at the top of his voice, saying 'Go away! What do You want with us, Jesus of Nazareth have you come to destroy us? I know who you are, the Holy One of God,' and Jesus said sternly, 'Be quiet and come out of him,' and then the demon threw the man down before them all and came out without injuring him" (Luke 4:33-35; Mark 1:23-27, NIV).

Jesus has power over demons: Matthew tells us the story about the demon possessed man that dwelled among the graves: "The demons begged Jesus, if you drive us out, send us into the pigs. Jesus said, 'Go,' so they came out and went into the pigs, and the pigs rushed down into the lake and died in the water" (Luke 8:26-39; Matt. 8:31-32, NIV). And a certain Gentile woman begged Jesus to heal her daughter, for she was severely tormented. Jesus was hesitant in the beginning, only testing her faith, but she said, "Even the dogs eat the crumbs that fall from their master's table.' Jesus said to her, 'Woman, you have great faith, your request is granted,' and her daughter was healed at that moment" (Matthew. 8:27-28, NIV).

Jesus came down from the mountain, and a certain man pleaded with Jesus to look on his son, for a spirit seizes him, convulses him so that he foams at his mouth, and leaves the child bruised. Jesus rebuked the unclean spirit, and the boy was healed and set free of the demon (Luke 9:37-42, NKJV).

Again, while "Jesus was in one of the synagogues on a Sabbath day, He saw a woman who had a spirit of infirmity for eighteen years, could not raise herself because she was bent over, then Jesus called her to Him and said, 'Woman, you are loosed from your infirmity.' Immediately, she was made straight and glorified God" (Luke 13:10-17, NKJV). Scripture tells us the people were amazed at the power and authority of Jesus as a deliverer.

TESTIMONY:

In one of my missions' trips to Qoas, Brazil, I visited a women's rehab center. After ministering to the individuals, deliverance took place whereby unclean spirits were cast out from them and from their rooms. Casting out unclean spirits also took place in Bangalore, India, where a spirit who dwelt in an older lady cried out, "Do not touch me, I have lived in her a long time, but I will come out from her," and the spirit left the lady.

Jesus as a Healer. The book of Luke tells us, "Jesus arose from the synagogue and entered

Simon's house, but found his mother lay sick and immediately Jesus rebuked the fever" (4:38-39; Mark 1:29-31, NKJV). Luke declares, when "the sun was setting Jesus healed various diseases and demons also came out of many crying out, 'You are the Christ, the Son of God'" (4:40-41; Mark 1:32-33, NKJV).

Again, Luke proclaims, a man filled with leprosy approached Jesus and begged Him to be healed, saying, "if You are willing, You can make me clean. Our loving Jesus said, I am willing, be cleansed" (5:12-13; Mark 1:40-42, NKJV).

Jesus is always moved with compassion, always willing to heal, with much pity, emotion, and love (Lamentation. 3:22-23; Mark:41).

Luke 5:17-26 affirms, a paralytic man was brought on a bed looking for Jesus "but because of the crowd the men went up on the housetop and let him down with his bed, when Jesus saw their faith, He declared the paralytic man healed, saying your sins are forgiven. I say to you arise, take up your bed and go to your house" (NKJV) (also reported in Mark 2:1-12).

Luke 14:1-6 declares, "Jesus was in the house of one of the rulers of the Pharisees to eat bread on a Sabbath and He met a man with dropsy. Jesus took him and healed Him."

How loving and caring is our Lord, who is the healer and deliverer and very compassionate! "While Jesus was on His way to Jerusalem He passed through the midst of Samaria and Galilee, ten lepers stood afar off in one of the villages and lifted their voices and said, 'Jesus, Master, have mercy on us.' Jesus saw them and said, 'Go, show yourselves to the priests,' and they were healed instantly" (Luke 17:11-19, NKJV)

Jesus met a certain blind man near Jericho who cried out to Him saying, "**Jesus, Son of David, have mercy on me.**" Jesus stood still and commanded him to be brought to Him. Jesus asked, "**What do you want me to do for you?**" The blind man said, "'Lord, that I may receive my sight.' Pleased with the blind man's faith, Jesus said, 'Receive your sight, your faith has made you well'" (Luke 18: 35-43; Mark 10:46-52, (NKJV). Hallelujah!

MY TESTIMONY:

I once mentored a new believer who did not know how to pray, and she needed to pray for her children, so I said, "Say: 'Jesus Son of the Most High God, have mercy on me and my children.'" It is a simple prayer and powerful. Jesus will surely turn around and stand. I also shared with her the story of the blind man by the roadside, how Jesus stopped and turned around.

TESTIMONY:

During one of my prayer sessions in one of the villages in Bangalore, India, a lady was carried to the Church because she could not walk; so, a belt was strapped around her waist, but after calling on Jesus our healer to have mercy on her, the lady was able to walk again. Jesus is a wondrous working Father. After the service, I was accompanied by the senior pastor of a church to one of his member's homes where I met a man who was paralyzed; after prayers, he too was healed instantly. What a wonder! Praise the Lord.

Most non-believers in some of the villages

in Bangalore, India, and most parts of the world accept Jesus as their personal Lord and Savior as soon as healing is performed, because whatever they worship cannot heal or deliver them from unclean spirits. So, as Christians, healing and deliverance is an excellent defense tool for our faith; it also helps to increase and strengthen the faith of believers.

Jesus blessed His servants with gifts. He said, "Very truly I tell you, whoever believes in me will do the works I have been doing, and they will do even greater things than these, because I am going to the Father" (John 14:12, NIV)

"Jesus entered Capernaum, and a centurion came to him, asking for help. Lord, my servant lies at home paralyzed, suffering terribly" (Matthew 8:5-6, NIV). Jesus healed him instantly.

Jesus has power over blindness: Scripture tells us, "When Jesus had gone indoors, certain blind men came to Him, asking for their eyes to be restored, and Jesus healed them of their blindness" (Matthew 9:28- 30, NIV).

Jesus as a miracle-worker and has power over wind

and water: "He got into the boat and His disciples followed Him, suddenly a furious storm came up on the lake, so that the waves swept over the boat, but Jesus was asleep, but the disciples went and woke Him, saying, 'Lord save us,' and Jesus rebuked the winds and the waves, and it was completely calm" (Matthew 8:23-26; Luke 8: 22-25, NIV).

"Jesus called His disciples and went to a deserted place belonging to a city called Bethsaida, but when the multitudes found out their location, they followed Him, but Jesus, filled with compassion, asked His disciples to provide food for them. With only five loaves of bread and two fish, Jesus asked that they sit down in groups of fifty. Jesus Christ looking up to heaven, blessed and broke the bread and fish. The five thousand ate and were filled, and twelve baskets of leftover fragments were taken up" (Luke 9:10-17; Matthew 14:13-21, NKJV)

Jesus has power over nature: "Jesus saw a fig tree by the road, He went up to it because He was hungry, but found nothing on it except leaves. Then He said to it, 'May you never bear fruit again,' and immediately the tree withered" (Matthew 21:18-19, NIV).

Jesus has power over history: "Jesus said, 'From now on you will see the Son of Man sitting at the right hand of the Mighty One and coming on the clouds of heaven'" (Matthew 26:64, NIV). Yes, Jesus Christ will return with great power and glory. Hallelujah!

Jesus has power over His own destiny: "Jesus began to explain to His disciples that He must go to Jerusalem and suffer many things at the hands of the elders, the chief priests and the teachers of the law, and that He must be killed and on the third day be raised to life" (Matthew16:21, NIV), and it was so.

Power over His mission on earth: "Jesus called the twelve disciples to Him and gave them authority to drive out impure spirits and to heal every disease and sickness" (Matthew 10:1, NIV)

Jesus has power over space, time, and the future: "Jesus said, 'Again, truly I tell you that if two of you on earth agree about anything they ask for, it will be done for them by My Father in heaven'" (Matthew18:19; 28:20, NIV).

Jesus as a healer and miracle worker: Luke tells

us, "Jesus entered the synagogue on a Sabbath day and restored a man with a withered right hand" (Luke 6:6-11; Mark 3:1-6, NKJV).

Jesus healed a woman with the issue of blood: "She spent what she had on physicians to be healed, but continued to suffer, until she encountered Jesus. By faith she touched the hem of Jesus's garment and was healed, but Jesus said, 'Who touched Me, for power has gone out of Me?'" (Matthew 9:20-22; Mark 5:25-34; Luke 8:43-48). Praise the Lord!

MY TESTIMONY:

For over ten years, I suffered much bleeding, and the doctor I visited said surgery would be the only solution (twenty-three centimeters of fibroids), but the Lord had mercy on me, and I was completely healed on the first week of September 2013. He said that carrying out His Will in my life is more important. The Lord also healed me of thyroiditis, diabetes, and high cholesterol and much more.

I once met a lady in a church at British Columbia, Canada, who was unable to stand during praise and worship because of much bleeding, but after prayers she was instantly healed.

A Lady in Canada who was unable to pick up a cup of coffee due to pain for almost two years was instantly healed after prayers.

Many wombs have been opened through prayers, doors were opened for businesses, and many more miracles have happened through prayers.

Luke 7:1-10 declares that Jesus healed a centurion's servant: "Jesus entered Capernaum, and there a centurion's servant, whom his master valued highly, was sick and about to die, and the centurion sent for Jesus, asking for his servant to be healed for the centurion is very deserving because of his kindness. So, Jesus offered to go, but the centurion said, 'I am not worthy, just say the word and my servant will be healed'" (NIV). Jesus was amazed, and his servant was healed. He is a miracle-worker. Do you have that kind of faith? Please pray for your faith to be increased.

Jesus has power over the dead: Luke declares, "Jesus entered a city called Nain, He met a dead man being carried out for burial, the only son of a widow, moved with compassion Jesus said, 'Do not weep,' then He touched the open coffin, and those who carried him stood still. Jesus said, 'Young man, I say to you, arise,' so, he who was dead sat up and began to speak" (7:11-17, NKJV).

A certain man named Jairus, a ruler of the synagogue, pleaded with Jesus for his daughter to be healed, but before Jesus could get to Jairus' home, the little girl was pronounced dead. Jesus said to those who wept, "Do not weep, she is not dead, but sleeping." Our loving Jesus said to the dead girl, "'Little girl, arise!' and the spirit entered her."

Jesus raises Lazarus from the dead: "Lazarus, the brother of Mary and Martha was dead for four days, but once again deeply moved, Jesus asked for the stone to be removed, saying 'Lazarus come out!' The dead man came out" (John 11:38-44, NIV).

The power of God is limitless; nothing is difficult for Him who created all things, "who stretched the heavens like a curtain" (Isaiah 40:22). "He brings forth the wind from His storehouses" (Jerimiah 51:16). Praise the Lord!

Jesus Christ was obedient to God the Father until the end. Jesus does whatever the Father says; the miracles of Jesus reveal His identity as God Himself at work. Indeed, God is encountered in the miracles, so the conclusion is that miracles identify Jesus as God. "The will of God in the lives of mankind is that we be made whole, that our souls also prosper" (3 John 1:2).

TESTIMONY:

As an evangelist, I met a young man in Bangalore, India, who was possessed with a spirit of dumbness. He asked for prayers regarding a job, but while we were praying, the spirit of dumbness manifested, and by the grace of God the spirit was expelled. I met him the following week, and he testified of God's goodness because he obtained an employment with the government of India.

I also experienced spirits of unforgiveness and anger on another occasion while praying for deliverance on an individual; a spirit of anger manifested in a rage, but Jesus is the Lord of Host, our Champion whose power is limitless.

Matthew 9: 32–33 (NIV) tells us
that Jesus healed the mute.

"Jesus as a miracle worker, commands His disciples not to carry a purse, no bags, no sandals, nor two tunics. Whatever house you enter, eat what is set before you, heal the sick and say to them, the kingdom of God has come upon you. This passage confirms that Jesus is a miracle worker." As the disciples went through cities and villages, they did not lack. With the power of God and faith in Jesus, the disciples left for evangelism, preaching the Kingdom of God, healing the sick and the oppressed, as commanded by Jesus our Lord. What an immense joy!

CHAPTER 20:

TYPOLOGY AND JESUS

ALSO CALLED ANTITYPE:

The Old Testament is brought to completion in Jesus, who is called Antitype.

THE BOOK OF MATTHEW CONNECTS JESUS WITH ISRAEL BY CITING HOSEA 11:1, WHICH SPEAKS OF GOD'S SON COMING OUT OF EGYPT:

Matthew shows that Jesus, like Israel of old, will be delivered from Egypt by God (See Matthew 2:15). Therefore, Israel is "a type" of Jesus (with Jesus as the "Antitype").

ANOTHER EXAMPLE: LET US CONSIDER THE TEMPLE IN JOHN'S GOSPEL.

Jesus fulfills the purposes of the temple: God's presence with His people (John 1:14-18). And according to John 2:13-22, Jesus could speak of His body as the temple. John also goes on to show that various Jewish festivals are types of Jesus' person and work. For instance, John understands the Feast of Tabernacle as Typological of Jesus' identity as light and the living water, key elements of this festival (John 8:12; 7:37-38).

THE TEMPTING OR TESTING OF JESUS IN THE WILDERNESS FOR FORTY YEARS HAS ITS PRIMARY BACKGROUND IN ISRAEL'S WILDERNESS EXPERIENCE IN DEUTERONOMY 6-8, IN WHICH JESUS QUOTES IN HIS THREE RESPONSES TO THE DEVIL'S TEMPTATIONS:

In Deuteronomy, Moses recalls how the Lord led the Israelites in the wilderness for forty years, "to humble and test you in order to know what was in your heart, whether or not you would keep His commandments" (Deuteronomy 8:2). At the beginning of Jesus' ministry, He was subject to similar test and shows Himself to be the True Israelite who "lives on every word that comes from the mouth of God" (Deu.8:3; Matthew 4:4). Israel failed the wilderness testing, but Jesus refused to bow down and worship the Devil and remained faithful to the One True God. Jesus overcomes temptation by clinging on to God; He used the word of God to defeat Satan.

IN GENESIS 22:1-14, ABRAHAM'S FAITH WAS TEMPTED WHEN GOD ASKED HIM TO SACRIFICE HIS ONLY SON ISAAC:

Abraham walked for three days to the region of Moriah where he was to sacrifice Isaac, and on the third day, he saw the place in the distance. Isaac asked his father, "'Where is the lamb?' And Abraham said God Himself will provide." An ultimate fulfillment is the Lamb of God. Abraham laid him on the altar, on top of the wood; Isaac here is a type of Christ. The author of Chronicles identified the place as the Temple Mount in Jerusalem (2 Chronicles 3:1). Today, Mount Moriah is occupied by the Dome of the Rock. Abraham's devotion is paralleled by God's love to us in Christ as reflected in John 3:16 and Romans 8:32.

MOSES WAS WITH THE LORD FORTY DAYS AND FORTY NIGHTS, WITHOUT EATING BREAD OR DRINKING WATER (EXODUS 34:28):

And Jesus was in the wilderness for forty days and forty nights without eating and drinking (Matthew 4:1-11).

IN THE OLD TESTAMENT:

When the Israelites worshiped the molded calf, 3,000 were wiped out, but in the New Testament, after Pentecost, 3,000 were added to the Church. **It is called Typology of Jesus.**

FOR THE JEWISH, IT IS THE 50TH DAY FROM THE TIME GOD DESCENDED ON MOUNT SANAI, WHERE FIRE, EARTHQUAKES, LIGHTNING, AND THUNDER OCCURRED (EXODUS 19:18, NKJV):

For the Christians, it is the 50th day before the Pentecost, for the people gathered on the day of Pentecost, and Peter told the people to repent and receive the Holy Spirit. Peter received the keys and started the Church, and Pentecost continues in the Church.

IN THE BOOK OF HEBREWS 13:11-12:

The bodies of those animals whose blood is brought into the Sanctuary by the High Priest for the sin are burnt outside the camp,

Therefore, Jesus also, that He might Sanctify the people with His own blood, suffered outside the gate.

Matthew 12:39-40 (NKJV):

Jesus answered and said to them, "An evil and adulterous generation seeks after a sign, and no sign will be given to it except the sign of the prophet Jonah. For as Jonah was three days and three nights in the belly of the great fish, so will the Son of Man be three days and three nights in the heart of the earth." Jesus rose on the third day. Hallelujah!

John 3:14-17:

"Just as Moses lifted the snake in the wilderness, so the Son of Man must be lifted, that everyone who believes may have eternal life in him.

"For God so loved the world that he gave his one and only Son, that whoever believes in him shall not perish but have eternal life. For God did not send his Son into the world to condemn the world, but to save the world through him" (NIV).

NOAH'S ARK, GENESIS 6:13-22:

Noah, his family, and the animals were protected and safe because Noah's Ark was the only way during the floods. But Jesus came in order for mankind to receive salvation, so all those who come to Jesus, who accept Jesus as their personal Savior, will be protected and safe because He is the only way to the Father, the only way to Heaven, where there is peace, bright light, order, discipline, love, compassion, joy, and gladness.

CHAPTER 21:

REVELATIONS

REVELATIONS: IN CONCLUSION

Regarding Praise, the Lord said:

I Am the giver of peace,

I Am the giver of Joy and gladness,

I Am the giver of comfort,

I Am the giver of healing and deliverance,

And the giver of wealth.

The Lord's desire is to lead us (His children) to Mount Zion.

Because in Mount Zion, there is holiness.

In Mount Zion, there is healing.

In Mount Zion, there is protection.

In Mount Zion, there is peace.

In Mount Zion, there is breakthrough.

In Mount Zion, there is favor.

In Mount Zion, there is abundance.

And in Mount Zion, there is deliverance.

CHAPTER 22

THE LORD'S DESIRE IS TO DELIVER MANKIND FROM THE TERRITORY OF THE ENEMIES TO OUR PROMISED LAND FOR BREAKTHROUGHS AND PEACE

DELIVERANCE:

PLEASE ALLOW THE LORD TO TAKE THE DRIVER'S SEAT IN YOUR LIFE:

The Lord will deliver you from the land of your enemies.

Jesus will part the Red Sea in your life.

He will provide for you.

He will part the River Jordan in your life.

The Lord will break down the walls of Jerico in your life and will destroy all your enemies.

He will destroy the Goliaths in your life, and you will sound the trumpets in praise.

But mankind must allow the Lord to take the driver's seat, for His ways are straight. He is the best Driver, Our Lord and God.

Amen!

BIBLIOGRAPHY

Carson, D. A. "Sin's Contemporary Significance," in Fallen: A Theology of Sin, eds. Christopher W. Morgan and Robert A. Peterson (Wheaton: Crossway, Inc., 24. 2013.

Zemek, "Hamartiology," in Syllabus, 40.

Ibid., 40. Zemek refers also to Edward J. Young Genesis 3 (London: Banner of Truth Trust. 60-61. 1996.

McFarland I.A. The Problem with Evil. Theology Today. 2018;74(4): 321-339.

Moody, Christopher. "Watch: The I AM Changes Who I Am" https://libertyuniversity.instructure.com/courses/318702/pages/watch-the-i-am-changes-who-i-am?module_item_id=36950928.

Morgan, W., & Peterson, R. A. What Is Sin? 1993.

Miller, Arthur. The Social Psychology of Good and Evil. New York: Guilford, 2004.

McFarland I.A. The Problem with Evil. Theology Today.74(4):321-339. 2018.

Pettit, Paul. Foundations of Spiritual Formation: A Community Approach to Becoming like Christ. Grand Rapids, MI: Kregel Publications, a division of Kregel, Inc., p.20,23. 2018.

Pereira, J. L. Augustine of Hippo and Martin Luther on original sin and justification of the sinner: Vandenhoeck & Ruprecht. 2003.

Pratt, J. B. The Ethics of St. Augustine. The International Journal of Ethics, 13(2), 222-235. 1903.

Keltz, B Kyle. "A Thomistic Answer to the Evil-God Challenge." The heythrop journal. 60.5 (2019): 689-698. Web.

Khaldoun A. Sweis and Chad V. Meister, Christian Apologetics: Anthology of Primary Sources. Grand Rapids, MI: Zondervan. 2012.

Plantinga, Alvin C. God, Freedom, and Evil. Grand Rapids, MI: William B. Eerdmans, 197.

Unless otherwise noted all biblical passages, refs implore the (NKJV) Nashville TN; Thomas Nelson, 1982.

"St. Hippo Augustine Argues. "The solution of evil is to do the right thing."

Chad Meister, "Augustine of Hippo: Apologist of Faith and Reason Seeking Understanding," in *The History of Apologetics*, ed. Benjamin K. Forrest, Joshua D. Chatraw, and Alister E. McGrath. Grand Rapids, MI: Zondervan Academic, 152. 2020.

Wenham, G. Original sin in Genesis 1-11. *Genesis, 1*, 11. 1990.